A cook's book of pasta

CARBONARA
MARINARA
NAPOLITANA

whitecap

This edition first published in Canada in 2006 by Whitecap Books, 351 Lynn Ave.,
North Vancouver, British Columbia, Canada, V7J 2C4.
www.whitecap.ca

First published by Murdoch Books Pty Limited in 2005.
www.murdochbooks.com.au

Chief Executive: Juliet Rogers
Publisher: Kay Scarlett

Design Manager: Vivien Valk
Design Concept, Design and Illustration: Alex Frampton
Project Manager: Janine Flew
Editor: Gordana Trifunovic
Introduction text: Leanne Kitchen
Recipes developed by the Murdoch Books Test Kitchen
Production: Monika Paratore

ISBN 1 55285 750 6
ISBN 978 1 55258 750 6

Printed by Midas Printing (Asia) Ltd in 2005. Printed in CHINA.

IMPORTANT: Those who might be at risk from the effects of salmonella poisoning (the
elderly, pregnant women, young children and those suffering from immune deficiency
diseases) should consult their doctor with any concerns about eating raw eggs.

CONVERSION GUIDE: You may find cooking times vary depending on the oven you are
using. For fan-forced ovens, as a general rule, set the oven temperature to 20°C (35°F)
lower than indicated in the recipe. We have used 20 ml (4 teaspoon) tablespoon measures.
If you are using a 15 ml (3 teaspoon) tablespoon, for most recipes the difference will
not be noticeable. However, for recipes using baking powder, gelatine, bicarbonate of
soda (baking soda) or small amounts of flour or cornflour (cornstarch), add an extra
teaspoon for each tablespoon specified.

A cook's book of pasta

CARBONARA
MARINARA
NAPOLITANA

Contents

versatile pasta

The Chinese and the Italians can argue all they like about who invented or discovered pasta, or who introduced it to the world, but thank goodness somebody did or for many of us, meal times would be a tad dull. From stretchy to stumpy, curvy to curly and flattened to filled, pasta comes in a fantastic range of forms. The most typical of Italian foods, pasta is not only amazingly versatile but is also a very good traveller too, insinuating itself onto lunch and dinner tables virtually everywhere to become universal fare.

The word pasta is, unromantically, simply the Italian word for 'paste' or 'dough' and in its most elemental, uncooked state, pasta is a smooth, firm amalgam of (mainly) flour and water or flour and egg yolks. It is shaped by rolling, or extruding, the paste into any one of literally hundreds of shapes, from supermarket staples such as macaroni, fettuccine and spaghetti, to an exotic-sounding assortment that includes conchiglie (shells), cappelini d'angelo (angel hair), rotelle (small, spoked wheels) and farfalle (bow-ties). It can be used in either its fresh state, where the delicate texture and subtle flavour best suit unfussy pairings, or dried, when more robust treatments and tastes are appropriate. Some pasta — such as gnocchi, which is based upon potato or ricotta or semolina — falls outside the basic formula, but such oddities are rare.

More common are the stuffed pastas, tender little savoury packages of which the best-known examples are tortellini and ravioli. The wonder of it is that, although fashioned from such ordinary ingredients, the array of dishes that can be created from pasta is seemingly limitless. Pasta loves a cream sauce, a cheesy sauce, a tomato sauce or a meaty sauce. It can just be boiled, tossed with a handful of this and a smattering of that then served in ten minutes flat, or it can be stuffed or layered and baked into a complex, crusty amalgam of rich textures and deep flavours. Soft strands of tagliatelle beg for seafood — octopus perhaps, or mussels, clams or prawns (shrimp). Vegetables were made for pasta; spinach, zucchini (courgette), mushrooms, beetroot and pumpkin (winter squash) are sublime when paired with any number of pasta shapes and some fresh herbs, garlic or a dollop of soft cheese. Endless meat and pasta possibilities exist; meatballs and the classic sauce bolognaise are obvious examples but chicken, veal and prosciutto are also prime candidates. Whatever one's preference though, if there's pasta in the pantry, a great meal is never very far away. Perhaps this is why the great Italian director Federico Fellini could so confidently declare life to be 'a combination of magic and pasta'.

Spaghetti with Meatballs Pasta Proscaiola

Pasta with meat

ic Lasagne Ravioli with Herbs Pasticcio

Spaghetti with Meatballs

Serves 4

MEATBALLS
500 g (1 lb 2 oz) ground (minced) beef
40 g (1$^{1}/_{2}$ oz/$^{1}/_{2}$ cup) fresh breadcrumbs
1 onion, finely chopped
2 garlic cloves, crushed
2 teaspoons worcestershire sauce
1 teaspoon dried oregano
30 g (1 oz/$^{1}/_{4}$ cup) plain (all-purpose) flour
2 tablespoons olive oil

SAUCE
800 g (1 lb 12 oz) tinned chopped tomatoes
1 tablespoon olive oil
1 onion, finely chopped
2 garlic cloves, crushed
2 tablespoons tomato paste (concentrated purée)
125 ml (4 fl oz/$^{1}/_{2}$ cup) beef stock
2 teaspoons sugar

500 g (1 lb 2 oz) spaghetti
grated parmesan cheese, to serve

1 Combine the ground beef, breadcrumbs, onion, garlic, worcestershire sauce and oregano in a bowl and season to taste. Mix well. Roll level tablespoons of the mixture into balls. Dust lightly with the flour and shake off the excess. Heat the oil in a deep frying pan and cook the meatballs in batches, turning frequently, until browned all over. Drain well.

2 To make the sauce, purée the tomatoes in a food processor or blender. Heat the oil in a frying pan. Add the onion and cook over medium heat for 2–3 minutes, or until soft and just lightly golden. Add the garlic and cook for a further 1 minute. Add the puréed tomatoes, tomato paste, stock and sugar to the pan and stir to combine. Bring the mixture to the boil, then add the meatballs. Reduce the heat and simmer for 15 minutes, turning the meatballs once. Season with salt and pepper.

3 Meanwhile, cook the spaghetti in a saucepan of boiling salted water until *al dente*. Drain, then divide among serving plates. Top with the meatballs and sauce. Serve with grated parmesan cheese.

Veal Tortellini with Baked Pumpkin and Basil Butter

Serves 4

1 kg (2 lb 4 oz) jap (kent) pumpkin (squash), cut into
   2 cm ($^3/_4$ in) cubes
600 g (1 lb 5 oz) veal tortellini
100 g ($3^1/_2$ oz) butter
3 garlic cloves, crushed
90 g ($3^1/_4$ oz/$^1/_2$ cup) pine nuts
45 g ($1^1/_2$ oz/$^2/_3$ cup) shredded basil
200 g (7 oz) feta cheese, crumbled

1 Preheat the oven to 220°C (425°F/Gas 7). Line a baking tray with baking paper. Place the pumpkin on the prepared tray and season well with salt and cracked black pepper. Bake for 30 minutes, or until the pumpkin is tender.

2 Meanwhile, cook the tortellini in a saucepan of boiling salted water until *al dente*. Drain and return to the saucepan to keep warm.

3 Heat the butter in a small frying pan over medium heat until foaming. Add the garlic and pine nuts and cook for 3–5 minutes, or until the nuts start to turn golden. Remove from the heat and add the basil. Toss the basil butter, pumpkin and feta through the tortellini and serve immediately.

Beef Vermicelli Cake

Serves 4-6

90 g (3¼ oz) butter
1 onion, chopped
500 g (1 lb 2 oz) ground (minced) beef
800 g (1 lb 12 oz) tomato pasta sauce
2 tablespoons tomato paste (concentrated purée)
250 g (9 oz) vermicelli
30 g (1 oz/¼ cup) plain (all-purpose) flour
310 ml (10¾ fl oz/1¼ cups) milk
150 g (5½ oz/1¼ cups) grated cheddar cheese

1   Preheat the oven to 180°C (350°F/Gas 4). Lightly grease a deep
    24 cm (10 in) round deep spring-form cake tin. Melt 20 g (¾ oz) of
    the butter in a frying pan and cook the onion over medium heat for
    2 minutes, or until soft. Add the beef and cook for 4 minutes, or until
    browned. Stir in the pasta sauce and tomato paste, reduce the heat
    and simmer for 20–25 minutes. Season well.

2   Cook the vermicelli in a saucepan of boiling salted water until
    al dente. Drain and rinse. Melt the remaining butter in a saucepan
    over low heat. Stir in the flour and cook for 1 minute, or until pale.
    Remove from the heat and stir in the milk. Return to the heat and
    stir until thickened. Reduce the heat and simmer for 2 minutes.

3   Spread half the pasta over the base of the tin, then cover with half
    the meat sauce. Cover with the remaining pasta. Spoon on the
    remaining meat sauce and then pour on the white sauce. Sprinkle
    with cheese and cook for 15 minutes. Leave to stand for 10 minutes
    before removing from the tin. Cut into wedges to serve.

Fusilli with Ham and Broccoli

Serves 4

400 g (14 oz) fusilli
250 g (9 oz) broccoli florets
30 g (1 oz) butter
250 g (9 oz) leg ham, cut into strips
2 garlic cloves, crushed
6 spring onions (scallions), chopped
200 g (7 oz) mushrooms, sliced
250 ml (9 fl oz/1 cup) thick (double/heavy) cream
2 handfuls chopped flat-leaf (Italian) parsley

1 Cook the fusilli in a saucepan of boiling salted water until *al dente*.
   Drain well and return to the pan to keep warm. Meanwhile, cook the
   broccoli in a saucepan of rapidly boiling water for 2 minutes or until
   tender, then drain.

2 Heat the butter in a large saucepan. Add the ham and stir over
   medium heat for 2 minutes or until lightly browned.

3 Add the garlic, spring onion and mushrooms and stir for 2 minutes.
   Add the pasta, broccoli, cream and parsley and stir for 1 minute to
   heat through.

 You can also add some cooked peas or
diced, cooked carrots.

Rigatoni with Kidney Beans and Italian Sausage

Serves 4-6

1 tablespoon olive oil
1 large onion, chopped
2 garlic cloves, crushed
4 Italian sausages, chopped
825 g (1 lb 11 oz) tinned crushed tomatoes
425 g (14 oz) tinned kidney or borlotti beans, drained
1 small handful chopped basil
1 small handful chopped sage
1 small handful chopped flat-leaf (Italian) parsley
500 g (1 lb 2 oz) rigatoni
grated parmesan cheese, to serve

1 Heat the oil in a medium heavy-based frying pan. Add the onion, garlic and sausage and cook, stirring occasionally, over medium heat for 5 minutes.

2 Add the tomatoes, beans, basil, sage and parsley and season well. Reduce the heat and simmer for 20 minutes.

3 Meanwhile, cook the rigatoni in a saucepan of boiling salted water until *al dente*. Drain and return to the saucepan to keep warm. Divide among serving bowls and top with the sauce. Sprinkle with parmesan cheese and serve immediately.

Tagliatelle with Ragù

Serves 4

60 g (2^{1}/$_{4}$ oz) butter
1 onion, finely chopped
1 celery stalk, finely chopped
1 carrot, finely chopped
90 g (3^{1}/$_{4}$ oz) pancetta or bacon, finely chopped
220 g (7^{3}/$_{4}$ oz) ground (minced) beef
220 g (7^{3}/$_{4}$ oz) ground (minced) pork
2 oregano sprigs, chopped
pinch of nutmeg
120 g (4 oz) chicken livers, trimmed and finely chopped
125 ml (4 fl oz/^{1}/$_{2}$ cup) dry white wine
215 ml (7^{1}/$_{2}$ fl oz) milk
400 g (14 oz) tinned chopped tomatoes
250 ml (9 fl oz/1 cup) beef stock
400 g (14 oz) tagliatelle
grated parmesan cheese, to serve

1 Heat the butter in a saucepan and add the onion, celery, carrot and pancetta. Cook, stirring occasionally, over medium heat for 6–8 minutes.

2 Add the beef, pork and oregano to the saucepan. Season with salt and pepper and the nutmeg. Cook for about 5 minutes, or until the ground beef and pork have changed colour but not browned. Add the chicken liver and cook until it changes colour.

3   Pour in the wine, increase the heat and boil over high heat for 2–3 minutes, or until the wine has been absorbed. Stir in 125 ml (4 fl oz/½ cup) of the milk, reduce the heat and simmer for 10 minutes. Add the tomatoes and half the stock, partially cover the pan and leave to simmer gently over low heat for 3 hours. Add more of the stock as it is needed to keep the sauce moist.

4   Cook the tagliatelle in a saucepan of boiling salted water until *al dente*. Stir the remaining milk into the sauce 5 minutes before serving and season to taste. Drain the pasta, toss with the sauce and serve with grated parmesan cheese.

Beef Sausage Fusilli

Serves 4

150 g (5½ oz) fusilli
4 thick beef sausages
2 tablespoons olive oil
1 large red onion, cut into wedges
250 ml (9 fl oz/1 cup) tomato pasta sauce
4 small ripe tomatoes, peeled, seeded and chopped
1 handful chopped flat-leaf (Italian) parsley

1 Cook the fusilli in a saucepan of boiling salted water until *al dente*. Drain and return to the pan to keep warm, reserving 60 ml (2 fl oz/ ¼ cup) of the cooking water.

2 Meanwhile, prick the sausages all over with a fork. Heat a non-stick frying pan and cook the sausages, turning often, over medium heat for 5 minutes, or until cooked. Cut into thick diagonal slices and set aside.

3 Wipe clean the frying pan and heat the oil. Cook the onion wedges over medium heat for 3 minutes, or until soft. Add the tomato pasta sauce and the tomato. Cook for 5 minutes, or until the tomato has softened. Add the sliced sausage and heat through for 1 minute.

4 Toss the pasta through the sauce, adding a little of the reserved pasta water, if necessary. Sprinkle with the parsley and serve immediately.

Conchiglie with Sausage and Tomato

Serves 4-6

500 g (1 lb 2 oz) conchiglie
2 tablespoons olive oil
400 g (14 oz) thin Italian sausages
1 red onion, finely chopped
2 garlic cloves, finely chopped
830 g (1 lb 13 oz) tinned chopped tomatoes
1 teaspoon caster (superfine) sugar
2 handfuls basil, torn
45 g ($1^{1}/2$ oz/$^{1}/2$ cup) grated pecorino cheese

1   Cook the conchiglie in a saucepan of boiling salted water until
    al dente. Drain and return to the pan to keep warm. Meanwhile,
    heat 2 teaspoons of the oil in a large frying pan. Add the sausages
    and cook, turning, for 5 minutes, or until well browned and cooked
    through. Drain on paper towels, then slice. Keep warm.

2   Wipe clean the frying pan and heat the remaining oil. Add the onion
    and garlic and cook over medium heat for 2 minutes, or until the
    onion has softened. Add the tomato, sugar and 250 ml (9 fl oz/1 cup)
    water and season well. Reduce the heat and simmer for 12 minutes,
    or until thickened and reduced a little.

3   Pour the sauce over the pasta and stir through the sausage, basil and
    half the cheese. Serve hot, sprinkled with the remaining cheese.

Macaroni Eggplant Bake

Serves 4–6

125 g (4¹/₂ oz) macaroni

2–3 eggplants (aubergines), sliced thinly lengthways

2 tablespoons olive oil, plus extra as needed

1 onion, chopped

1 garlic clove, crushed

500 g (1 lb 2 oz) ground (minced) beef

425 g (15 oz) tinned crushed tomatoes

2 tablespoons tomato paste (concentrated purée)

150 g (5¹/₂ oz/¹/₂ cup) frozen peas

150 g (5¹/₂ oz/1 cup) grated mozzarella cheese

60 g (2¹/₄ oz/¹/₂ cup) grated cheddar cheese

1 egg, beaten

60 g (2¹/₄ oz/¹/₂ cup) grated parmesan cheese

1   Grease and line a deep 23 cm (9 in) round spring-form cake tin. Cook the macaroni in a saucepan of boiling salted water until *al dente*. Drain and return to the pan to keep warm.

2   Put the eggplant in a colander and sprinkle generously with salt. Leave for 20 minutes, then rinse well. Pat dry with paper towels. Heat the oil in a frying pan and fry the eggplant in batches in a single layer until golden on each side. Add more oil as required. Drain on paper towels.

3   Add the onion and garlic to the frying pan and stir over low heat until tender. Add the beef and cook until browned. Add the tomato, tomato paste and salt and pepper and stir well. Bring to the boil. Reduce the heat and simmer for 15–20 minutes, then set aside.

4   Mix together the peas, macaroni, mozzarella and cheddar cheeses, egg and half the parmesan.

5   Preheat the oven to 180°C (350°F/Gas 4). Place a slice of eggplant in the centre of the tin. Arrange three-quarters of the remaining eggplant in an overlapping pattern to completely cover the base and side of the tin. Sprinkle with half the remaining parmesan cheese.

6   Combine the beef with the macaroni mixture. Carefully spoon the filling into the eggplant shell, packing it down well. Arrange the remaining eggplant slices, overlapping, over the filling. Sprinkle with the remaining parmesan cheese.

7   Bake for 25–30 minutes or until golden. Leave for 5 minutes before unmoulding onto a serving plate.

Penne with Rosemary and Prosciutto

Serves 4–6

1 tablespoon olive oil

6 thin slices prosciutto, chopped

1 onion, finely chopped

825 g (1 lb 13 oz) tinned crushed tomatoes

1 tablespoon chopped rosemary

500 g (1 lb 2 oz) penne

50 g (1¹/₂ oz/¹/₂ cup) grated parmesan cheese, to serve

1 Heat the oil in a heavy-based frying pan. Add the prosciutto and onion and cook, stirring occasionally, over low heat for 5 minutes or until the prosciutto is golden and the onion has softened.

2 Add the tomato, rosemary and salt and pepper to the pan and simmer for 10 minutes.

3 Meanwhile, cook the pasta in a saucepan of boiling salted water until *al dente*. Drain and return to the pan to keep warm. Divide among serving bowls and top with the sauce. Sprinkle with parmesan cheese and serve immediately.

Rosemary, commonly used in Mediterranean cookery, adds a distinctive flavour to this dish.

Spaghetti Pizzaiola

Serves 4

2 tablespoons olive oil
2 garlic cloves, crushed
250 g (9 oz) ground (minced) beef or veal
850 g (1 lb 14 oz) tinned tomatoes
125 ml (4 fl oz/1/2 cup) red wine
1 tablespoon chopped capers
1/2 teaspoon dried marjoram
1/2 teaspoon dried basil
2 tablespoons chopped flat-leaf (Italian) parsley
500 g (1 lb 2 oz) spaghetti

1 Heat the oil in a frying pan, add the garlic and stir over low heat for 1 minute. Add the mince and brown well, breaking up with a fork as it cooks.

2 Add the tomatoes, wine, capers, marjoram and basil and season with salt and pepper. Bring to the boil. Reduce the heat and simmer for 20 minutes, or until the sauce is reduced by half. Add the parsley and stir well.

3 Meanwhile, cook the spaghetti in a saucepan of boiling salted water until *al dente*. Drain and return to the pan to keep warm. Add the sauce and toss together. Serve immediately.

Pappardelle with Salami, Leek and Provolone Cheese

Serves 4

375 g (13 oz) pappardelle
2 tablespoons olive oil
2 leeks, thinly sliced
2 tablespoons white wine
800 g (1 lb 12 oz) tinned diced tomatoes
150 g (5 1/2 oz) sliced mild salami, cut into strips
1 small handful basil leaves, torn
125 g (4 1/2 oz) provolone cheese, sliced into strips
30 g (1 oz) grated parmesan cheese

1 Cook the pappardelle in a saucepan of boiling salted water until *al dente*. Drain and return to the pan to keep warm.

2 Meanwhile, heat the oil in a large deep frying pan. Add the leek and cook over low heat for 4 minutes, or until soft but not browned. Increase the heat to medium, add the wine and stir until almost evaporated.

3 Add the tomato and salami, season with salt and cracked black pepper and simmer for 5 minutes, or until reduced slightly. Toss the tomato sauce mixture, basil and provolone lightly through the pasta. Sprinkle with parmesan cheese and serve immediately.

Mediterranean Spaghetti

Serves 4

140 ml (4³/4 fl oz) olive oil
1 teaspoon dried oregano
2 garlic cloves, finely chopped
6 roma (plum) tomatoes, halved
500 g (1 lb 2 oz) spaghetti
4 slices prosciutto
16 kalamata olives
200 g (7 oz) feta cheese, cut into bite-size cubes
1 tablespoon balsamic vinegar
3 garlic cloves, thinly sliced, extra
60 g (2¹/4 oz) rocket (arugula) leaves, trimmed

1 Preheat the oven to150°C (300°F/Gas 2). Combine 2 tablespoons of the olive oil, the oregano, garlic and 1 teaspoon salt in a bowl. Add the tomato and toss well. Put the tomato cut-side-up on a baking tray and cook in the oven for 1 hour.

2 Meanwhile, cook the pasta in a saucepan of boiling salted water until *al dente*. Drain and return to the pan to keep warm. Grill (broil) the prosciutto under a hot grill (broiler), turning once, for 3–4 minutes, or until crisp. Break into pieces.

3 Toss the tomato, olives, feta, spaghetti and balsamic vinegar in a bowl and keep warm.

4 Heat the remaining olive oil in a saucepan and cook the extra garlic over low heat for 1–2 minutes.

5 Pour the garlic and oil over the spaghetti mixture, add the rocket leaves and toss well. Add the prosciutto pieces and season.

Baked Meatballs and Macaroni

Serves 4

100 g (3¹/₂ oz) macaroni
500 g (1 lb 2 oz) ground (minced) beef
1 onion, finely chopped
2 tablespoons grated parmesan cheese
1 tablespoon chopped basil
1 egg, beaten
90 g (3¹/₄ oz/1 cup) fresh breadcrumbs
2 tablespoons olive oil
150 g (5¹/₂ oz/1 cup) grated mozzarella cheese

SAUCE
1 onion, sliced
1 garlic clove, crushed
1 capsicum (pepper), seeded and sliced
125 g (4¹/₂ oz) mushrooms, sliced
60 g (2¹/₄ oz) tomato paste (concentrated purée)
125 ml (4 fl oz/¹/₂ cup) red wine

1 Cook the macaroni in a saucepan of boiling salted water until
   al dente. Drain and return to the pan to keep warm. Mix together
   the mince, onion, parmesan, basil, egg and half the breadcrumbs.
   Form heaped teaspoons of the mixture into balls.

2 Heat the oil in a frying pan and cook the meatballs until well
   browned. Drain on paper towels. Transfer to an ovenproof dish.
   Preheat the oven to 180°C (350°F/Gas 4).

3 To make the sauce, add the onion and garlic to the frying pan and stir over low heat until tender. Add the capsicum and mushrooms and cook for 2 minutes. Stir in the tomato paste. Add 250 ml (9 fl oz/1 cup) of water and the wine and bring to the boil. Mix in the macaroni and salt and pepper. Pour over the meatballs.

4 Bake for 30–35 minutes. Sprinkle with the mozzarella cheese and remaining breadcrumbs. Bake for a further 10 minutes, or until golden.

Spaghetti Boscaiola

Serves 4

500 g (1 lb 2 oz) spaghetti
1 tablespoon olive oil
6 bacon slices, chopped
200 g (7 oz) button mushrooms, sliced
625 ml (21 fl oz/2¹/2 cups) pouring cream
2 spring onions (scallions), sliced
1 tablespoon chopped flat-leaf (Italian) parsley

1 Cook the spaghetti in a saucepan of boiling salted water until *al dente*. Drain and return to the pan to keep warm.

2 Meanwhile, heat the oil in a large frying pan. Add the bacon and mushrooms and cook, stirring, for 5 minutes, or until golden brown. Add a little of the cream and stir well with a wooden spoon.

3 Add the remaining cream, bring to the boil and cook over high heat for 15 minutes or until thick enough to coat the back of a spoon. Add the spring onions. Pour the sauce over the pasta and toss well. Serve sprinkled with the parsley.

This sauce is normally served with spaghetti, but you can use any pasta. If you are short on time and don't have 15 minutes to reduce the sauce, it can be thickened with 2 teaspoons of cornflour mixed with 1 tablespoon of water. Stir until the mixture boils and thickens.

Veal Agnolotti with Alfredo Sauce

serves 4–6

625 g (1 lb 6 oz) veal agnolotti
90 g (3¼ oz) butter
150 g (5½ oz/1½ cups) grated parmesan cheese
300 ml (10½ fl oz) pouring cream
2 tablespoons chopped marjoram

1 Cook the agnolotti in a saucepan of boiling salted water until *al dente*. Drain and return to the pan to keep warm.

2 Meanwhile, melt the butter in a saucepan over low heat. Add the parmesan and cream and bring to the boil. Reduce the heat and simmer, stirring constantly, for 2 minutes or until the sauce has thickened slightly. Stir in the marjoram and season with salt and cracked black pepper. Toss the sauce through the pasta and serve immediately.

Marjoram can be replaced with any other fresh herb you prefer — try parsley, thyme, chervil or dill.

Rigatoni with Chorizo and Tomato

Serves 4

2 tablespoons olive oil

1 onion, sliced

250 g (9 oz) chorizo sausage, sliced

425 g (14 oz) tinned crushed tomatoes

125 ml (4 fl oz/$1/2$ cup) dry white wine

$1/2$–1 teaspoon chopped chilli, optional

375 g (13 oz) rigatoni

1 small handful chopped flat-leaf (Italian) parsley, to serve

40 g ($1^1/2$ oz) grated parmesan cheese, to serve

1 Heat the oil in a frying pan. Add the onion and stir over low heat until tender.

2 Add the sausage to the frying pan and cook, turning frequently, for 2–3 minutes. Add the tomatoes, wine and chilli and season with salt and pepper. Bring to the boil, reduce the heat and simmer for 15–20 minutes.

3 Meanwhile, cook the pasta in a saucepan of boiling salted water until *al dente*. Drain and return to the pan to keep warm. Add the sauce to the pasta with half the combined parsley and parmesan cheese. Toss well. Serve sprinkled with the remaining combined parsley and parmesan cheese.

Creamy Veal and Mushroom Pappardelle

Serves 4

100 g (3¹/₂ oz) butter
500 g (1 lb 2 oz) veal schnitzel, cut into bite-sized pieces
300 g (10¹/₂ oz) Swiss brown mushrooms, sliced
3 garlic cloves, crushed
185 ml (6 fl oz/³/₄ cup) dry white wine
125 ml (4 fl oz/¹/₂ cup) chicken stock
200 ml (7 fl oz) thick (double/heavy) cream
1–2 tablespoons lemon juice
400 g (14 oz) pappardelle

1   Melt half the butter in a large frying pan over medium heat. Add the veal in batches and cook for 2–3 minutes, or until golden brown. Remove the veal from the pan and keep warm.

2   Add the remaining butter to the same pan and heat until foaming. Add the mushrooms and garlic and cook, stirring, over low heat for 5 minutes. Pour in the wine and stock, scraping the bottom of the pan with a wooden spoon, and simmer, covered, for 10 minutes.

3   Remove the lid, add the cream and simmer for 5 minutes, or until the sauce thickens. Stir in the lemon juice, veal and any juices until warmed through. Season to taste.

4   Meanwhile, cook the pappardelle in a saucepan of boiling salted water until *al dente*. Drain, toss the sauce through the pasta and serve immediately.

Classic Lasagne

Serves 4-6

250 g (9 oz) lasagne sheets

75 g (1¹/2 oz/¹/2 cup) grated mozzarella cheese

60 g (2 oz/¹/2 cup) grated cheddar cheese

125 ml (4 fl oz/¹/2 cup) pouring cream

60 g (2¹/4 oz) grated parmesan cheese

CHEESE SAUCE

60 g (2¹/4 oz) butter

40 g (1¹/4 oz/¹/3 cup) plain (all-purpose) flour

500 ml (17 fl oz/2 cups) milk

125 g (4¹/2 oz/1 cup) grated cheddar cheese

MEAT SAUCE

1 tablespoon olive oil

1 onion, finely chopped

1 garlic clove, crushed

500 g (1 lb 2 oz) ground (minced) beef

850 g (1 lb 14 oz) tinned tomatoes

60 ml (2 fl oz/¹/4 cup) red wine

¹/2 teaspoon ground oregano

¹/4 teaspoon ground basil

1 Preheat the oven to180°C (350°F/Gas 4). Lightly grease a 24 x 30 cm (9¹/2 x 12 in) shallow ovenproof dish. Line with lasagne sheets, breaking them to fill any gaps.

2 To make the cheese sauce, melt the butter in a saucepan. Add the flour and stir for 1 minute. Remove from the heat and slowly add the

milk, stirring until smooth. Return to the heat and cook, stirring, over medium heat until the sauce boils and thickens. Reduce the heat and simmer for 3 minutes. Stir in the cheese, season and set aside.

3   To make the meat sauce, heat the oil in a large saucepan. Add the onion and garlic and stir over low heat until the onion is tender. Add the ground beef and brown well, breaking it up with a fork as it cooks. Stir in the tomato, wine, oregano, basil and salt and pepper. Bring to the boil, reduce the heat and simmer for 20 minutes.

4   Spoon one-third of the meat sauce over the lasagne sheets. Top with one-third of the cheese sauce. Arrange another layer of lasagne sheets over the top.

5   Repeat with two more layers of each. Top with the remaining lasagne sheets, then sprinkle with the combined mozzarella and cheddar cheeses. Pour the cream over the top. Sprinkle with the parmesan cheese. Bake for 35–40 minutes, or until golden.

Creamy Conchiglie with Peas and Prosciutto

serves 4

100 g (3¹/2 oz) thinly sliced prosciutto
3 teaspoons oil
2 eggs
250 ml (9 fl oz/1 cup) pouring cream
35 g (1 oz/¹/3 cup) finely grated parmesan cheese
1 small handful chopped flat-leaf (Italian) parsley
1 tablespoon chopped chives
250 g (9 oz) fresh or frozen peas
500 g (1 lb 2 oz) conchiglie

1　Cut the prosciutto into thin strips. Heat the oil in a frying pan over medium heat. Add the prosciutto and cook for 2 minutes, or until crisp. Drain on paper towels. Whisk together the eggs, cream, parmesan cheese and herbs in a large bowl.

2　Bring a large saucepan of salted water to the boil. Add the peas and cook for 5 minutes, or until just tender. Leaving the pan on the heat, use a slotted spoon and transfer the peas to the bowl of cream mixture, and then add 3 tablespoons of the cooking liquid to the same bowl. Using a potato masher or the back of a fork, roughly mash the peas.

3　Add the pasta to the boiling water and cook until *al dente*. Drain and return to the pan to keep warm. Add the cream mixture, then warm through over low heat, gently stirring until the pasta is coated in the sauce. Season to taste. Divide among serving plates, top with the prosciutto and serve.

Bucatini with Sausage and Fennel Seed

Serves 4

500 g (1 lb 2 oz) Italian sausages
2 tablespoons olive oil
3 garlic cloves, chopped
1 teaspoon fennel seeds
1/2 teaspoon chilli flakes
850 g (1 lb 14 oz) tinned crushed tomatoes
500 g (1 lb 2 oz) bucatini
1 teaspoon balsamic vinegar
1 small handful basil, chopped

1   Heat a frying pan over high heat, add the sausages and cook, turning, for 8–10 minutes, or until well browned and cooked through. Remove, cool slightly and slice thinly on the diagonal.

2   Heat the oil in a saucepan, add the garlic and cook over medium heat for 1 minute. Add the fennel seeds and chilli flakes and cook for a further minute. Stir in the tomato and bring to the boil, then reduce the heat and simmer, covered, for 20 minutes.

3   Meanwhile, cook the pasta in a saucepan of boiling salted water until *al dente*. Drain and return to the pan to keep warm.

4   Add the sausages to the sauce and cook, uncovered, for 5 minutes to heat through. Stir in the balsamic vinegar and basil. Divide the pasta among serving bowls, top with the sauce and serve.

Ravioli with Herbs

Serves 4–6

2 tablespoons olive oil
1 garlic clove, halved
800 g (1 lb 10 oz) ravioli
60 g (2¼ oz) butter, chopped
1 small handful chopped flat-leaf (Italian) parsley
20 g (¾ oz/⅓ cup) chopped basil
1 small handful chopped chives

1 Combine the oil and garlic in a small bowl and set aside.

2 Cook the ravioli in a saucepan of boiling salted water until *al dente*. Drain and return to the pan to keep warm.

3 Add the oil to the pasta, discarding the garlic. Add the butter and herbs and toss well. Serve immediately.

Penne with Creamy Tomato and Bacon Sauce

Serves 4

400 g (14 oz) penne
1 tablespoon olive oil
180 g (6 oz) bacon slices
500 g (1 lb 2 oz) roma (plum) tomatoes, roughly chopped
125 ml (4 fl oz/½ cup) thick (double/heavy) cream
2 tablespoons sun-dried tomato pesto
1 small handful finely chopped flat-leaf (Italian) parsley
50 g (1¾ oz/½ cup) finely grated parmesan cheese

1 Cook the penne in a saucepan of boiling salted water until *al dente*. Drain and return to the pan to keep warm.

2 Meanwhile, heat the oil in a frying pan. Add the bacon and cook over high heat for 2 minutes, or until starting to brown. Reduce the heat to medium, add the tomato and cook, stirring frequently, for 2 minutes, or until the tomato has softened.

3 Add the cream and tomato pesto and stir until heated through. Remove from the heat, add the parsley, then toss the sauce through the pasta with the parmesan cheese.

Pasticcio

Serves 4–6

60 ml (2 fl oz/$^1/_4$ cup) olive oil

1 onion, finely chopped

2 garlic cloves, crushed

90 g (3$^1/_4$ oz) pancetta, finely chopped

500 g (1 lb 2 oz) ground (minced) beef

1 teaspoon chopped oregano

60 g (2$^1/_4$ oz) button mushrooms, sliced

120 g (4 oz) chicken livers, trimmed and finely chopped

$^1/_2$ teaspoon ground nutmeg

$^1/_2$ teaspoon cayenne pepper

60 ml (2 fl oz/$^1/_4$ cup) dry white wine

2 tablespoons tomato paste (concentrated purée)

375 ml (12 fl oz/1$^1/_2$ cups) beef stock

140 g (5 oz/1$^1/_3$ cups) grated parmesan cheese, extra

2 eggs, beaten

150 g (5$^1/_2$ oz) macaroni

100 g (3$^1/_2$ oz) ricotta cheese

2 tablespoons milk

BECHAMEL SAUCE

40 g (1$^1/_4$ oz) butter

1$^1/_2$ tablespoons plain (all-purpose) flour

pinch of ground nutmeg

300 ml (10$^1/_2$ fl oz) milk

1 bay leaf

1   Preheat the oven to 180°C (350°F/Gas 4). Lightly grease a 1.5 litre (52 fl oz/6 cup) ovenproof dish. Heat the oil in a large frying pan

over medium heat. Cook the onion, garlic and pancetta, stirring, for 5–6 minutes, or until the onion is golden. Add the beef, increase the heat and stir for 5 minutes, or until the meat is browned.

2 Add the oregano, mushrooms, chicken livers and half the nutmeg and cayenne. Season and cook for 2 minutes. Add the wine and cook over high heat for 1 minute. Stir in the tomato paste and stock. Reduce the heat and simmer for 45 minutes, or until thickened. Beat 40 g (1½ oz) of the parmesan and the egg together and quickly stir through.

3 Cook the macaroni in a saucepan of boiling salted water until *al dente*. Drain and return to the pan to keep warm. Meanwhile, blend the ricotta, milk, extra egg, 25 g (1 oz) of the parmesan and the remaining cayenne and nutmeg. Season. Drain the macaroni, add to the ricotta mixture and mix well.

4 To make the béchamel sauce, melt the butter in a small saucepan. Stir in the flour and cook over low heat until beginning to turn golden, then stir in the nutmeg. Remove from the heat and gradually stir in the milk. Add the bay leaf and season. Return to low heat and simmer, stirring, until thickened. Discard the bay leaf.

5 Spread half the meat sauce in the dish, layer half the pasta over the top and sprinkle with half the remaining parmesan. Layer with the remaining meat sauce and pasta. Press down firmly with the back of a spoon. Spread the béchamel over the top and sprinkle with the remaining parmesan. Bake for 45–50 minutes until golden. Rest for 15 minutes before serving.

Fusilli with Bacon and Broad Bean Sauce

Serves 4–6

500 g (1 lb 2 oz) fusilli
300 g (10¹/2 oz/2 cups) frozen broad beans
2 tablespoons olive oil
2 leeks, finely sliced
4 bacon slices, diced
315 ml (10³/4 fl oz/1¹/4 cups) pouring cream
2 teaspoons grated lemon zest

1 Cook the fusilli in a saucepan of boiling salted water until *al dente*. Drain and return to the pan to keep warm.

2 Meanwhile, put the broad beans into a saucepan of boiling water. Remove with a slotted spoon and place immediately in cold water. Drain and allow to cool, then peel (see note).

3 Heat the oil in a heavy-based frying pan. Add the leek and bacon and cook, stirring occasionally, over medium heat for 8 minutes, or until the leek is golden. Add the cream and lemon zest and cook for 2 minutes. Add the broad beans and season well.

4 Add the sauce to the pasta and toss to combine. Serve at once.

Broad beans can be cooked and peeled in advance and refrigerated in an airtight container until needed. To peel them, break off the top and squeeze out the beans.

Penne with Sun-dried Tomatoes and Lemon

Serves 4

250 g (9 oz) penne
60 ml (2 fl oz/¼ cup) olive oil
3 bacon slices, chopped
1 onion, chopped
80 ml (2¾ fl oz/⅓ cup) lemon juice
1 tablespoon thyme leaves
50 g (1¾ oz/⅓ cup) chopped sun-dried tomatoes
90 g (3¼ oz/½ cup) pine nuts, toasted

1. Cook the penne in a saucepan of boiling salted water until *al dente*. Drain and return to the pan to keep warm.

2. Heat the oil in a large saucepan. Add the bacon and onion and stir over medium heat for 4 minutes, or until the bacon is brown and the onion has softened. Add the pasta, lemon juice, thyme, tomato and pine nuts. Stir over low heat for 2 minutes to heat through.

 Use pancetta instead of bacon, if preferred.

Rich Beef and Mushroom Lasagne

Serves 8

1 tablespoon olive oil
2 garlic cloves, crushed
1 onion, chopped
1 carrot, grated
1 celery stalk, diced
125 g (4^{1}/$_{2}$ oz) mushrooms, chopped
600 g (1 lb 5 oz) ground (minced) beef
600 ml (21 fl oz) tomato passata (puréed tomatoes)
1 teaspoon dried oregano leaves
300 g (10^{1}/$_{2}$ oz) instant lasagne sheets
100 g (3^{1}/$_{2}$ oz/1 cup) grated parmesan cheese

CHEESE SAUCE
60 g (2^{1}/$_{4}$ oz) butter
40 g (1^{1}/$_{2}$ oz/^{1}/$_{3}$ cup) plain (all-purpose) flour
1 litre (35 fl oz/4 cups) milk
^{1}/$_{2}$ teaspoon ground nutmeg
125 g (4^{1}/$_{2}$ oz/1 cup) grated cheddar cheese

1 Heat the oil in a large heavy-based frying pan. Add the garlic, onion, carrot, celery and mushroom. Cook, stirring, over medium heat for 2–3 minutes, or until the onion has softened. Increase the heat, add the ground beef and stir for a further 3–4 minutes, or until the beef has browned and is well broken up.

2 Add the tomato passata, oregano and 500 ml (17 fl oz/2 cups) of water. Bring to the boil, stirring, then lower the heat and simmer for 1 hour, or until the mixture has thickened. Stir occasionally.

3 To make the cheese sauce, melt the butter in a heavy-based saucepan. Add the flour and cook, stirring, for 1 minute until pale and foaming. Remove from the heat, gradually add the milk and stir until smooth. Return to the heat and stir continuously for 3–4 minutes, or until the sauce boils and thickens. Cook over low heat for 1 minute. Stir in the nutmeg and cheddar cheese. Season.

4 Preheat the oven to 180°C (350°F/Gas 4). Grease a 2.5 litre (87 fl oz/10 cup) baking dish. Arrange four lasagne sheets over the base of the baking dish. Spread one-third of the meat mixture over the sheets, then pour over about 185 ml (6 fl oz/3/4 cup) of the cheese sauce. Repeat with two more layers of each. Top with the four remaining lasagne sheets, then with the remaining sauce and finish with the parmesan cheese. Bake for 45 minutes, or until golden. Leave to stand for 5 minutes before serving.

Agnolotti with Creamy Tomato Sauce and Bacon

Serves 4

4 bacon slices
625 g (1 lb 6 oz) veal or chicken agnolotti
1 tablespoon olive oil
2 garlic cloves, finely chopped
120 g (4 oz/²/₃ cup) thinly sliced semi-dried tomatoes
1 tablespoon chopped thyme
375 ml (12 fl oz/1¹/₂ cups) pouring cream
1 teaspoon finely grated lemon zest
30 g (1 oz/¹/₃ cup) grated parmesan cheese

1   Grill (broil) the bacon for 5 minutes on each side, or until crisp and golden. Drain on paper towels and then break into pieces.

2   Cook the agnolotti in a saucepan of boiling salted water until *al dente*. Drain well and return to the pan to keep warm. Heat the oil in a frying pan and cook the garlic over medium heat for 1 minute, or until just golden. Add the semi-dried tomatoes and thyme and cook for 1 minute.

3   Add the cream, bring to the boil, then reduce the heat and simmer for 6–8 minutes, or until thickened and reduced by one-third. Season and add the lemon zest and 2 tablespoons of the parmesan cheese. Serve over the pasta, topped with the remaining parmesan and bacon pieces. Serve immediately.

Farfalle with Spinach and Bacon

Serves 4

400 g (14 oz) farfalle
2 tablespoons extra virgin olive oil
250 g (9 oz) bacon slices, chopped
1 red onion, finely chopped
250 g (9 oz) baby English spinach leaves
1–2 tablespoons sweet chilli sauce
30 g (1 oz/¼ cup) crumbled feta cheese

1. Cook the farfalle in a saucepan of boiling salted water until *al dente*. Drain and return to the pan to keep warm.

2. Meanwhile, heat the oil in a frying pan, add the bacon and cook over medium heat for 3 minutes, or until golden. Add the onion and cook for a further 4 minutes, or until softened. Toss the spinach leaves through the onion and bacon mixture for 30 seconds, or until just wilted.

3. Add the bacon and spinach mixture to the drained pasta, then stir in the sweet chilli sauce. Season to taste with salt and cracked black pepper and toss well. Spoon into bowls and scatter with the crumbled feta. Serve immediately.

Bocconcini, Prosciutto and Spinach Lasagne

serves 4–6

600 g (1 lb 5 oz) tomato pasta sauce
250 g (9 oz) fresh lasagne sheets
400 g (14 oz) bocconcini (fresh baby mozzarella cheese), thinly sliced
500 g (1 lb 2 oz) English spinach, trimmed
125 ml (4 fl oz/1/2 cup) pouring cream
10 thin slices prosciutto, chopped
150 g (51/2 oz/1 cup) grated mozzarella cheese
60 g (21/4 oz/1/2 cup) grated parmesan cheese

1 Preheat the oven to 180°C (350°F/Gas 4). Lightly grease a shallow
3 litre (104 fl oz/12 cup) ovenproof dish. Spread half of the tomato
pasta sauce over the base of the dish. Cover with a third of the
lasagne sheets. Top with half of the bocconcini and half of the
spinach. Drizzle on half of the cream and sprinkle with half of the
prosciutto. Season well. Repeat with two more layers of each.

2 Lay the final layer of lasagne over the top and spread with the
remaining pasta sauce. Sprinkle with the mozzarella and parmesan
cheeses. Bake for 25 minutes, or until cooked. Allow to stand for
10 minutes before serving.

Baked Spaghetti Frittata

Serves 4

30 g (1 oz) butter
125 g (4½ oz) mushrooms, sliced
1 capsicum (pepper), seeded and chopped
125 g (4½ oz) ham, sliced
90 g (3¼ oz/½ cup) frozen peas
6 eggs
250 ml (9 fl oz/1 cup) pouring cream or milk
100 g (3½ oz) cooked spaghetti, chopped
1 small handful chopped flat-leaf (Italian) parsley
60 g (2¼ oz/½ cup) grated parmesan cheese

1   Preheat the oven to 180°C (350°F/Gas 4). Grease a 23 cm (9 in) flan dish. Melt the butter in a frying pan and add the mushrooms. Cook over low heat for 2–3 minutes.

2   Add the capsicum and cook for 1 minute. Stir in the ham and peas. Remove from the heat to cool slightly.

3   Whisk together the eggs and cream and some salt and pepper. Add the spaghetti, parsley and mushroom mixture and stir. Pour into the dish and sprinkle with parmesan cheese. Bake for 25–30 minutes.

Beef and Spinach Cannelloni

Serves 4–6

FILLING

1 tablespoon olive oil

1 onion, chopped

1 garlic clove, crushed

500 g (1 lb 2 oz) ground (minced) beef

250 g (9 oz) frozen English spinach, thawed

60 g (2¼ oz) tomato paste (concentrated purée)

125 g (4½ oz/½ cup) ricotta cheese

1 egg

½ teaspoon ground oregano

BECHAMEL SAUCE

250 ml (9 fl oz/1 cup) milk

1 sprig flat-leaf (Italian) parsley

5 peppercorns

30 g (1 oz) butter

1 tablespoon plain (all-purpose) flour

125 ml (4 fl oz/½ cup) pouring cream

TOMATO SAUCE

425 g (15 oz) tomato paste (concentrated purée)

1 small handful chopped basil

1 garlic clove, crushed

½ teaspoon sugar

12–15 instant cannelloni tubes

150 g (5½ oz/1 cup) grated mozzarella cheese

60 g (2¼ oz/½ cup) grated parmesan cheese

1. Preheat the oven to 180°C (350°F/Gas 4). Lightly grease a large shallow ovenproof dish. To make the filling, heat the oil in a frying pan. Add the onion and garlic and stir over low heat until the onion is tender. Add the ground beef and brown well, breaking up any lumps with a fork as it cooks. Add the spinach and tomato paste. Cook, stirring, for 1 minute. Remove from the heat. Mix together the ricotta, egg, oregano and some salt and pepper. Add to the beef mixture and stir well.

2. To make the béchamel sauce, put the milk, parsley and peppercorns in a small saucepan. Bring to the boil. Remove from the heat and cool for 10 minutes. Strain, discarding the flavourings. Melt the butter in a small pan and stir in the flour. Cook, stirring, for 1 minute. Remove from the heat. Gradually blend in the strained milk, stirring until smooth. Return to the heat and cook, stirring constantly, over medium heat until the sauce boils and thickens. Reduce the heat and simmer for 3 minutes. Add the cream and season.

3. To make the tomato sauce, put all the ingredients in a pan and bring to the boil. Reduce the heat and simmer for 5 minutes.

4. Spoon the filling into a piping bag and fill the cannelloni tubes (or fill with a teaspoon).

5. Spoon a little of the tomato sauce in the base of the dish. Arrange the cannelloni on top.

6. Pour béchamel sauce over the cannelloni, followed by the remaining tomato sauce. Sprinkle the combined cheeses over the top. Bake for 30–35 minutes, or until golden.

Risoni-Filled Capsicums

Serves 4-6

1 tablespoon olive oil

1 onion, finely chopped

1 garlic clove, crushed

3 bacon slices, finely chopped

150 g (5^1/$_2$ oz) risoni, cooked

150 g (5^1/$_2$ oz/1 cup) grated mozzarella cheese

60 g (2^1/$_4$ oz/^{1}/$_2$ cup) grated parmesan cheese

1 small handful chopped flat-leaf (Italian) parsley

4 large red capsicums (peppers), halved lengthways, seeds removed

425 g (14 oz) tinned crushed tomatoes

125 ml (4 fl oz/^{1}/$_2$ cup) dry white wine

1 tablespoon tomato paste (concentrated purée)

^{1}/$_2$ teaspoon ground oregano

2 tablespoons chopped basil

1 Preheat the oven to 180°C (350°F/Gas 4). Lightly grease a large shallow ovenproof dish. Heat the oil in a frying pan and cook the onion and garlic over low heat until tender. Add the bacon and stir until crisp.

2 Transfer to a large bowl and add the risoni, cheeses and parsley. Spoon into the capsicum halves and arrange in the dish.

3 Combine the tomatoes, wine, tomato paste and oregano. Season and spoon over the risoni mixture. Sprinkle with basil. Bake for 35–40 minutes.

Baked Cannelloni Milanese

Serves 4

500 g (1 lb 2 oz) ground (minced) pork and veal
60 g (2¼ oz/½ cup) dry breadcrumbs
120 g (4 oz/1 cup) grated parmesan cheese
2 eggs, beaten
1 teaspoon dried oregano
12–15 cannelloni tubes
375 g (13 oz) ricotta cheese
60 g (2¼ oz/½ cup) grated cheddar cheese

TOMATO SAUCE
425 g (15 oz) tinned crushed tomatoes
425 g (15 oz) tinned tomatoes
2 garlic cloves, crushed
15 g (½ oz/¼ cup) chopped basil

1 Preheat the oven to 180°C (350°F/Gas 4). Lightly grease a shallow ovenproof dish. Mix together the pork and veal, breadcrumbs, half the parmesan cheese, the beaten egg, oregano and some salt and pepper. Use a teaspoon to stuff the mixture into the cannelloni tubes.

2 To make the tomato sauce, put the tomatoes and garlic in a saucepan and bring to the boil. Reduce the heat and simmer for 15 minutes. Add the basil and some black pepper and stir well.

3 Spoon half the sauce over the base of the dish. Arrange the cannelloni tubes on top of the sauce. Cover with the remaining sauce. Spread with the ricotta and sprinkle with the cheddar and remaining parmesan. Bake, covered with foil, for 1 hour. Uncover and bake for another 15 minutes or until golden. Cut into squares to serve.

Pork and Veal Ravioli with Cheesy Sauce

Serves 4

DOUGH

250 g (9 oz/2 cups) plain (all-purpose) flour

2 eggs, lightly beaten

2 tablespoons oil

FILLING

1 tablespoon oil

4 spring onions (scallions), finely chopped

3 garlic cloves, crushed

250 g (9 oz) ground (minced) pork and veal

1 egg, lightly beaten

SAUCE

60 g (2 1/4 oz) butter

220 g (7 3/4 oz/1 cup) mascarpone cheese

35 g (1 1/4 oz/1/3 cup) freshly grated parmesan cheese

2 tablespoons chopped sage

1. To make the dough, combine the flour, beaten eggs and oil with 80 ml (2 3/4 fl oz/1/3 cup) of water in a food processor for 5 seconds, or until the mixture comes together in a ball. Cover with plastic wrap and refrigerate for 15 minutes. Alternatively, combine the ingredients in a large bowl, using your fingertips.

2. To make the filling, heat the oil in a heavy-based frying pan, add the spring onion and garlic and stir-fry over medium heat for 2 minutes. Add the pork and veal and stir-fry, breaking up any lumps with a fork

as it cooks, over high heat for 4 minutes or until well browned. Allow to cool and stir in the egg.

3   Roll half the dough out very thinly on a lightly floured surface. Use a large sharp knife to cut the dough into 6 cm (2½ in) squares. Brush half the squares very lightly with water and place a teaspoon of filling on each. Place another square over each and press down firmly to seal the filling inside. Place in a single layer on well-floured baking trays. Repeat with the remaining dough and filling.

4   To make the sauce, melt the butter in a saucepan, add the mascarpone cheese and stir over medium heat until melted. Add the parmesan cheese and sage and gently heat, stirring, for 1 minute.

5   Cook the ravioli in a saucepan of boiling salted water until *al dente*. Drain and serve with the sauce.

Prosciutto and Sweet Potato Penne

Serves 4

500 g (1 lb 2 oz) penne
500 g (1 lb 2 oz) orange sweet potato, diced
2 tablespoons extra virgin olive oil
5 spring onions (scallions), sliced
2 garlic cloves, crushed
8 thin slices prosciutto, chopped
125 g (4¹/2 oz) sun-dried tomatoes in oil, drained and sliced
1 handful shredded basil leaves

1 Cook the penne in a saucepan of boiling salted water until *al dente*. Drain and return to the pan to keep warm.

2 Meanwhile, steam the sweet potato for 5 minutes, or until tender. Heat the oil in a saucepan, add the spring onion, garlic and sweet potato and stir over medium heat for 2–3 minutes, or until the spring onion is soft. Add the prosciutto and tomato and cook for a further 1 minute.

3 Add the sweet potato mixture to the penne and toss over low heat until heated through. Add the basil and season with black pepper. Serve immediately.

Fettucine Carbonara

Serves 4-6

8 bacon slices
500 g (1 lb 2 oz) fettucine
4 eggs
315 ml (10 fl oz/1¼ cups) pouring cream
60 g (2 oz/½ cup) grated parmesan cheese, plus extra to serve

1   Remove the bacon rind and cut the bacon into thin strips. Cook in a frying pan over medium heat until crisp. Drain on paper towels.

2   Meanwhile, cook the fettucine in a saucepan of boiling salted water until *al dente*. Drain and return to the pan to keep warm.

3   Beat the eggs, cream and parmesan together and season well. Stir in the bacon. Pour over the hot pasta in the saucepan and toss gently until the sauce coats the pasta. Return to very low heat and cook for about 1 minute, or until the sauce has thickened slightly. Season with black pepper and serve immediately with extra parmesan cheese.

Potato Gnocchi with Pancetta and Sage Sauce

Serves 4

1 kg (2 lb 4 oz) floury potatoes, unpeeled
2 egg yolks
2 tablespoons grated parmesan cheese
125–185 g (4¹/2–6¹/2 oz) plain (all-purpose) flour

SAUCE
20 g (³/4 oz) butter
75 g (2¹/2 oz) pancetta or bacon, cut into thin strips
8 small sage or basil leaves
150 ml (5 fl oz) thick (double/heavy) cream
50 g (1³/4 oz) parmesan cheese, grated

1   Prick the potatoes all over, then bake for 1 hour, or until tender. Leave to cool for 15 minutes, then peel and mash.

2   Mix in the egg yolks and parmesan, then gradually stir in the flour. When the mixture gets too dry to use a spoon, work with your hands. Once a loose dough forms, transfer to a lightly floured surface and knead gently. Work in enough extra flour to give a soft, pliable dough that is damp to the touch but not sticky.

3   Divide the dough into six portions. Working with one portion at a time, roll out on the floured surface to make a rope about 1.5 cm (⁵/8 in) thick. Cut the rope into 1.5 cm (⁵/8 in) lengths. Take one piece of dough and press your finger into it to form a concave shape, then roll the outer surface over the tines of a fork to make

deep ridges. Fold the outer lips in towards each other to make a hollow in the middle. Continue with the remaining dough.

4   Bring a large saucepan of salted water to the boil. Add the gnocchi in batches, about 20 at a time. Stir gently and return to the boil. Cook for 1–2 minutes, or until they rise to the surface. Remove with a slotted spoon, drain and put in a greased shallow casserole or baking tray. Preheat the oven to 200°C (400°F/Gas 6).

5   To make the sauce, melt the butter in a small deep frying pan and fry the pancetta until crisp. Stir in the sage leaves and cream. Season and simmer for 10 minutes, or until thickened.

6   Pour the sauce over the gnocchi, toss gently and sprinkle the parmesan on top. Bake for 10–15 minutes, or until the parmesan melts and turns golden. Serve hot.

Spaghetti with Salami and Capsicum

Serves 4-6

2 tablespoons olive oil

1 large onion, finely chopped

2 garlic cloves, crushed

150 g (5¹/₂ oz) spicy salami slices, cut into strips

2 large red capsicums (peppers), chopped

825 g (1 lb 13 oz) tinned crushed tomatoes

125 ml (4 fl oz/¹/₂ cup) dry white wine

1 teaspoon dried basil

500 g (1 lb 2 oz) spaghetti

1 Heat the oil in a heavy-based frying pan. Add the onion, garlic and salami and cook, stirring, for 5 minutes over medium heat. Add the capsicum, cover the pan and cook for 5 minutes.

2 Add the crushed tomatoes, wine and basil. Bring to the boil, then reduce the heat and simmer, covered, for 15 minutes.

3 Uncover the pan and simmer for another 15 minutes, or until the sauce has thickened slightly. Season well.

4 Meanwhile, cook the spaghetti in a saucepan of boiling salted water until *al dente*. Drain and toss with the sauce to serve.

Ditalini with Borlotti Beans

Serves 4

200 g (7 oz) dried borlotti beans
2 tablespoons olive oil
100 g (3 1/2 oz) pancetta, diced
1 celery stalk, chopped
1 onion, finely chopped
1 carrot, diced
1 garlic clove, crushed
1 large handful chopped flat-leaf (Italian) parsley
1 bay leaf
400 g (14 oz) tinned chopped tomatoes, drained
1.5 litres (52 fl oz/6 cups) vegetable stock
150 g (5 1/2 oz) ditalini
extra virgin olive oil, to drizzle
grated parmesan cheese, to serve

1   Place the beans in a large saucepan, cover with cold water and soak overnight. Drain and rinse under cold water.

2   Heat the olive oil in a large saucepan and add the pancetta, celery, onion, carrot and garlic and cook over low heat for 5 minutes, or until golden. Season with black pepper. Add the parsley, bay leaf, tomatoes, stock and borlotti beans and bring slowly to the boil. Reduce the heat and simmer for 1–1 1/2 hours, or until the beans are tender, adding a little boiling water every so often to maintain the level of liquid.

3   Add the ditalini and simmer for about 6 minutes, or until *al dente*. Remove from the heat. Divide among serving bowls and drizzle with extra virgin olive oil. Serve the parmesan cheese separately.

Low-fat Lasagne

Serves 8

2 teaspoons olive oil

1 large onion, chopped

2 carrots, finely chopped

2 celery stalks, finely chopped

2 zucchini (courgettes), finely chopped

2 garlic cloves, crushed

500 g (1 lb 2 oz) ground (minced) lean beef

800 g (1 lb 12 oz) tinned crushed tomatoes

125 ml (4 fl oz/^{1}/$_2$ cup) beef stock

40 g (1^1/$_2$ oz) tomato paste (concentrated purée)

2 teaspoons dried oregano

375 g (13 oz) lasagne sheets

CHEESE SAUCE

750 ml (24 fl oz/3 cups) low-fat milk

40 g (1^1/$_2$ oz/^{1}/$_3$ cup) cornflour (cornstarch)

100 g (3^1/$_2$ oz) reduced-fat cheese, grated

1   Heat the olive oil in a large non-stick frying pan. Add the onion and cook for 5 minutes, or until soft. Add the carrot, celery and zucchini and cook, stirring constantly, for 5 minutes, or until the vegetables are soft. Add the crushed garlic and cook for a further 1 minute. Add the ground beef and cook over high heat, stirring, until well browned. Break up any lumps of meat with a wooden spoon.

2   Add the crushed tomato, beef stock, tomato paste and dried oregano to the pan and stir to combine. Bring the mixture to the boil, then

reduce the heat and simmer gently, partially covered, for 20 minutes, stirring occasionally to prevent the mixture sticking to the pan.

3   Preheat the oven to 180°C (350°F/Gas 4). Spread a little of the meat sauce into the base of a 23 x 30 cm (9 x 12 in) ovenproof dish. Arrange a layer of lasagne sheets in the dish, breaking some of the sheets, if necessary, to fit in neatly.

4   Spread half the meat sauce over the top to cover evenly. Cover with another layer of lasagne sheets, a layer of meat sauce, then a final layer of lasagne sheets.

5   To make the cheese sauce, blend a little of the milk with the cornflour, to form a smooth paste, in a small saucepan. Gradually blend in the remaining milk and stir constantly over low heat until the mixture boils and thickens. Remove from the heat and stir in the grated cheese until melted. Spread evenly over the top of the lasagne and bake for 1 hour.

6   Check the lasagne after 25 minutes. If the top is browning too quickly, cover loosely with non-stick baking paper or foil. To serve, cut the lasagne into eight portions.

This lasagne can be frozen for up to 2–3 months. When required, thaw overnight in the refrigerator, then reheat, covered with foil, for about 30 minutes in a 180°C (350°F/Gas 4) oven.

Bucatini All'amatriciana

serves 4

1 tablespoon olive oil
150 g (5 1/2 oz) pancetta, in 2 thick slices
1 small onion, finely chopped
2 garlic cloves, crushed
3/4 teaspoon dried chilli flakes
600 g (1 lb 5 oz) tinned chopped tomatoes
400 g (14 oz) bucatini
1 handful finely chopped flat-leaf (Italian) parsley
grated parmesan cheese, to serve

1   Heat the oil in a large saucepan. Trim the fat from the pancetta and add the fat to the pan. Cook the pancetta fat over medium–high heat until it is crisp to extract the liquid fat, then discard the rinds. Dice the pancetta, add to the saucepan and cook until lightly browned.

2   Add the onion and fry for about 6 minutes, or until soft. Add the garlic and chilli flakes and cook, stirring, for 15–20 seconds then stir in the tomatoes. Season with salt and pepper. Simmer the sauce for about 15 minutes, or until it thickens and darkens.

3   Meanwhile, cook the bucatini in a saucepan of boiling salted water until *al dente*. Drain the pasta. Stir the parsley into the sauce, toss together with the pasta and serve with parmesan cheese.

Classic Spaghetti Bolognese

Serves 4

50 g (1³/4 oz) butter
180 g (6¹/2 oz) thick bacon slices, with rind removed, finely chopped
1 large onion, finely chopped
1 carrot, finely chopped
1 celery stick, finely chopped
400 g (14 oz) ground (minced) lean beef
150 g (5¹/2 oz) chicken livers, finely chopped
500 ml (17 fl oz/2 cups) beef stock
250 g (9 oz) tinned crushed tomatoes
125 ml (4 fl oz/¹/2 cup) red wine
¹/4 teaspoon freshly grated nutmeg
500 g (1 lb 2 oz) spaghetti
grated parmesan cheese, for serving

1 Heat half the butter in a heavy-based frying pan. Add the bacon and cook until golden. Add the onion, carrot and celery and cook over low heat for 8 minutes, stirring often.

2 Increase the heat, add the remaining butter and, when the pan is hot, add the beef, breaking up any lumps with a fork as it cooks. Add the chicken livers and stir until they change colour. Add the beef stock, crushed tomatoes, wine and nutmeg and season to taste.

3 Bring to the boil and then reduce the heat and simmer, covered, over very low heat for 2–5 hours, adding more stock if the sauce becomes too dry. The longer the sauce is cooked, the more flavour it will have.

4 Cook the spaghetti in a saucepan of boiling salted water until *al dente*. Drain and serve with the sauce and parmesan cheese.

Ziti with Sausage

Serves 4

1 red capsicum (pepper)
1 green capsicum (pepper)
1 small eggplant (aubergine), sliced
60 ml (2 fl oz/¼ cup) olive oil
1 onion, sliced
1 garlic clove, crushed
250 g (9 oz) chipolata sausages, sliced
425 g (14 oz) tinned crushed tomatoes
125 ml (4 fl oz/½ cup) red wine
60 g (2¼ oz) halved pitted black olives
1 small handful chopped basil
1 small handful chopped flat-leaf (Italian) parsley
500 g (1 lb 2 oz) ziti
40 g (1½ oz) grated parmesan cheese, to serve

1   Cut both capsicums into large flat pieces, removing the seeds and membranes. Place under a hot grill (broiler) until the skin blackens and blisters. Cover with a damp tea towel and then peel off the skin. Chop and set aside.

2   Brush the eggplant with a little of the oil. Grill (broil) until golden on each side, brushing with more oil as required. Set aside.

3   Heat the remaining oil in a frying pan. Add the onion and garlic and stir over low heat until the onion is tender. Add the chipolatas and cook until well browned. Stir in the tomatoes, wine, olives, basil, parsley and salt and pepper. Bring to the boil. Reduce the heat and simmer for 15 minutes. Add the vegetables and heat through.

4 Meanwhile, cook the ziti in a saucepan of boiling salted water until
   al dente. Drain and return to the pan to keep warm. Toss the
   vegetables and sauce through the hot pasta. Sprinkle with parmesan
   cheese before serving.

Smoked Chicken Linguine Chicken Carb

Pasta with chicken

Chicken Agnolotti Pesto Chicken Penne

Fettucine with Chicken and Mushroom Sauce

Serves 4

400 g (14 oz) fettucine
2 large chicken breast fillets
1 tablespoon olive oil
30 g (1 oz) butter
2 bacon slices, chopped
2 garlic cloves, crushed
250 g (9 oz) button mushrooms, sliced
80 ml (2³/4 fl oz/¹/3 cup) white wine
170 ml (5¹/2 fl oz/²/3 cup) pouring cream
4 spring onions (scallions), chopped
1 tablespoon plain (all-purpose) flour
35 g (1¹/4 oz/¹/3 cup) grated parmesan cheese, to serve

1 Cook the fettucine in a saucepan of boiling salted water until *al dente*. Drain and return to the pan to keep warm.

2 Meanwhile, trim the chicken of excess fat and cut into thin strips. Heat the oil and butter in a heavy-based frying pan. Add the chicken and cook over medium heat for 3 minutes, or until browned. Add the bacon, garlic and mushrooms and cook for 2 minutes.

3 Add the wine and cook until the liquid has reduced by half. Add the cream and spring onion and bring to the boil. Blend the flour with a little water until smooth, add to the pan and stir until the mixture thickens. Reduce the heat and simmer for 2 minutes. Season to taste.

4 Add the sauce to the pasta and stir over low heat until combined. Sprinkle with parmesan cheese.

Chicken and Eggplant Penne

Serves 4

375 g (13 oz) penne
100 ml (3¹/₂ fl oz) olive oil
4 slender eggplants (aubergines), thinly sliced on the diagonal
2 chicken breast fillets
2 teaspoons lemon juice
2 handfuls chopped flat-leaf (Italian) parsley
270 g (9¹/₂ oz) chargrilled red capsicum (pepper), drained and sliced
150 g (5¹/₂ oz) asparagus, trimmed, blanched and cut into short lengths
90 g (3¹/₄ oz) semi-dried tomatoes, finely sliced
grated parmesan cheese, to serve

1 Cook the penne in a saucepan of boiling salted water until *al dente*. Drain and return to the pan to keep warm.

2 Meanwhile, heat 2 tablespoons of the oil in a large frying pan over high heat and cook the eggplant for 4–5 minutes, or until golden and cooked through.

3 Heat a lightly oiled chargrill pan over high heat and cook the chicken for 5 minutes each side, or until browned and cooked through. Cut into thick slices. Combine the lemon juice, parsley and the remaining oil in a small jar and shake well. Return the pasta to the heat, toss through the dressing, chicken, eggplant, capsicum, asparagus and tomato until well mixed and warmed through. Season with black pepper and serve with parmesan cheese.

Chicken and Spinach Lasagne

Serves 8

500 g (1 lb 2 oz) English spinach
1 kg (2 lb 4 oz) ground (minced) chicken
1 garlic clove, crushed
3 bacon slices, chopped
425 g (15 oz) tinned crushed tomatoes
125 g (4^1/$_2$ oz/^{1}/$_2$ cup) tomato paste (concentrated purée)
125 g (4^1/$_2$ oz/^{1}/$_2$ cup) tomato pasta sauce
125 ml (4 fl oz/^{1}/$_2$ cup) chicken stock
12 instant lasagne sheets
125 g (4^1/$_2$ oz/1 cup) grated cheddar cheese

CHEESE SAUCE
60 g (2^1/$_4$ oz) butter
40 g (1^1/$_4$ oz/^{1}/$_3$ cup) plain (all-purpose) flour
600 ml (21 fl oz/2^1/$_2$ cups) milk
125 g (4^1/$_2$ oz/1 cup) grated cheddar cheese

1 Preheat the oven to 180°C (350°F/Gas 4). Remove and discard the stalks from the spinach leaves. Plunge the leaves in a saucepan of boiling water for 2 minutes, or until tender. Remove, plunge immediately into a bowl of iced water and then drain.

2 Heat a little oil in a heavy-based frying pan. Add the chicken, garlic and bacon. Cook over medium heat for 5 minutes, or until browned. Stir in the tomato, tomato paste, sauce and stock and bring to the boil. Reduce the heat and simmer, partially covered, for 10 minutes, or until the sauce is slightly thickened. Season with salt and pepper, to taste.

3   To make the cheese sauce, melt the butter in a saucepan, add the flour and stir over low heat for 1 minute, or until the mixture is lightly golden and smooth. Remove from the heat and gradually stir in the milk. Return to the heat and stir constantly over medium heat for 4 minutes, or until the sauce boils and thickens. Remove from the heat and stir in the cheese.

4   To assemble the lasagne, lightly grease a deep 3 litre (104 fl oz/ 12 cup) ovenproof dish. Spread one-quarter of the chicken mixture over the base. Top with 4 sheets of lasagne. Spread with one-third of the cheese sauce, then another layer of the chicken filling. Top with all of the spinach, a layer of lasagne, a layer of cheese sauce and the remaining chicken filling. Spread evenly with the remaining cheese sauce and sprinkle with the grated cheese. Bake for 50 minutes, or until cooked through and golden brown.

Chicken Pasta Bake

Serves 4

200 g (7 oz) fusilli
425 g (15 oz) tinned cream of mushroom soup
250 g (9 oz/1 cup) sour cream
1 teaspoon curry powder
1 barbecued chicken
250 g (9 oz) broccoli, cut into small pieces
90 g (3¼ oz/1 cup) fresh breadcrumbs
185 g (6½ oz/1½ cups) grated cheddar cheese

1   Preheat the oven to 180°C (350°F/Gas 4). Cook the fusilli in a saucepan of boiling salted water until *al dente*. Drain and return to the pan to keep warm.

2   Combine the soup, sour cream and curry powder and season to taste with freshly ground black pepper.

3   Remove the meat from the chicken and roughly chop. Combine the chicken with the pasta, broccoli and soup mixture. Spoon into four lightly greased 500 ml (17 fl oz/2 cup) ovenproof dishes and sprinkle with the combined breadcrumbs and cheese. Bake for 25–30 minutes, or until the cheese melts.

This recipe can be made in a 2 litre (70 fl oz/8 cup) ovenproof dish and baked for 40 minutes, or until the cheese has melted.

Smoked Chicken Linguine

Serves 4

1 tablespoon olive oil
1 leek, thinly sliced
3 large garlic cloves, finely chopped
125 ml (4 fl oz/$\frac{1}{2}$ cup) dry white wine
300 g (10$\frac{1}{2}$ oz) Swiss brown mushrooms, sliced
2 teaspoons chopped thyme
300 ml (10$\frac{1}{2}$ fl oz) thick (double/heavy) cream
2 smoked chicken breast fillets, thinly sliced
350 g (12 oz) linguine

1   Heat the oil in a saucepan. Add the leek and cook, stirring, over low heat for 3–4 minutes, or until soft. Add the garlic and cook for a further 1 minute. Pour in the wine and simmer for 2–3 minutes, or until the liquid has reduced by half.

2   Increase the heat to medium, add the mushrooms and thyme and cook for 5 minutes, or until any excess liquid has been absorbed. Add the cream and sliced chicken. Reduce the heat and simmer for 4–5 minutes, or until the sauce has slightly thickened.

3   Meanwhile, cook the linguine in a saucepan of boiling salted water until *al dente*. Drain and divide among serving plates. Spoon on the sauce and serve.

Chicken and Pumpkin Cannelloni

Serves 6

FILLING

500 g (1 lb 2 oz) butternut pumpkin (squash), with skin and seeds

30 g (1 oz) butter, melted

100 g (3¹/2 oz) pancetta, roughly chopped

2 teaspoons olive oil

2 garlic cloves, crushed

500 g (1 lb 2 oz) ground (minced) chicken

¹/2 teaspoon garam masala

1 small handful flat-leaf (Italian) parsley, chopped

150 g (5¹/2 oz) goat's cheese

50 g (1³/4 oz) ricotta cheese

375 g (13 oz) fresh lasagne sheets

100 g (3¹/2 oz/1 cup) grated parmesan cheese

SAUCE

30 g (1 oz) butter

1 garlic clove, crushed

850 g (1 lb 14 oz) tinned crushed tomatoes

1 handful flat-leaf (Italian) parsley, chopped

60 ml (2 fl oz/¹/4 cup) white wine

1 Preheat the oven to 220°C (425°F/Gas 7). Brush the pumpkin with 10 g (¹/4 oz) of the butter and bake on a baking tray for 1 hour, or until tender. When the pumpkin has cooked and while it is still hot, remove the seeds. Scrape out the flesh and mash it with a fork. Set aside to cool.

2 Add another 10 g (¼ oz) of the butter to a heavy-based frying pan and cook the pancetta over medium heat for 2–3 minutes. Remove from the pan and drain on paper towels.

3 In the same pan, heat the remaining butter and olive oil. Add the garlic and stir for 30 seconds. Add the chicken in small batches and brown, making sure the chicken is cooked through. Set aside to cool. Reduce the oven temperature to 200°C (400°F/Gas 6).

4 Combine the pumpkin with the pancetta and chicken in a bowl. Mix in the garam marsala, parsley, goat's cheese, ricotta and some salt and black pepper. Cut the lasagne sheets into rough 15 cm (6 in) squares. Place 3 tablespoons of the filling evenly along the length of the square, then roll up. Repeat with the rest of the lasagne sheets and filling.

5 To make the tomato sauce, melt the butter in a heavy-based frying pan and add the garlic. Cook for 1 minute, add the tomatoes and simmer over medium heat for 1 minute. Add the parsley and white wine and simmer gently for another 5 minutes. Season, to taste.

6 Spread a little of the tomato sauce in a 3 litre (104 fl oz/12 cup) ovenproof dish and arrange the cannelloni on top in a single layer. Spoon the remaining tomato sauce over the cannelloni and sprinkle with parmesan. Bake for 20–25 minutes, or until the cheese is golden.

You can use instant cannelloni tubes instead of lasagne. Stand the tubes on end on a chopping board and spoon in the filling.

Chicken and Macaroni Bake

Serves 6

4 chicken breast fillets

310 g (11 oz/2 cups) macaroni elbows

60 ml (2 fl oz/1/4 cup) olive oil

1 onion, chopped

1 carrot, chopped

3 bacon slices, chopped

2 zucchini (courgettes), chopped

440 g (15 1/2 oz) tinned tomato soup

90 g (3 1/4 oz/1/3 cup) sour cream

185 g (6 1/2 oz/1 1/2 cups) grated cheddar cheese

1   Trim the chicken of excess fat and sinew. Preheat the oven to 180°C (350°F/Gas 4). Cook the macaroni in a saucepan of boiling salted water until *al dente*. Drain.

2   Meanwhile, slice the chicken breasts into long strips and then cut into cubes. Heat the oil in a heavy-based pan. Cook the chicken quickly over high heat until browned but not cooked through. Drain on paper towels. Add the onion, carrot and bacon to the pan. Stir over medium heat for 10 minutes. Add the zucchini and soup, bring to the boil and simmer for 5 minutes. Remove from the heat.

3   Combine the pasta, chicken, tomato mixture and sour cream. Season with salt and pepper, to taste. Spread into a shallow ovenproof dish and top with cheese. Bake for 20 minutes, or until golden and cooked through.

Lasagnette with Chicken and Mushrooms

serves 4

60 ml (2 fl oz/1/4 cup) milk
2 teaspoons chopped tarragon
400 g (14 oz) lasagnette
25 g (1 oz) butter
2 garlic cloves
200 g (7 oz) chicken breast fillet, sliced
100 g (3 1/2 oz) button mushrooms, thinly sliced
pinch of ground nutmeg
500 ml (17 fl oz/2 cups) pouring cream

1 Bring the milk and tarragon to the boil in a small pan. Remove from the heat, strain and reserve the milk. Set aside.

2 Cook the lasagnette in a saucepan of boiling salted water until *al dente*. Drain and return to the pan to keep warm.

3 Meanwhile, melt the butter in a frying pan and gently sauté the whole garlic cloves, sliced chicken and button mushrooms until the chicken is golden and cooked through. Discard the garlic cloves, add the nutmeg and season to taste. Stir for 10 seconds before stirring in the cream and tarragon milk. Bring to the boil, reduce the heat and simmer until the sauce thickens. Spoon the sauce over the pasta and serve immediately.

Spaghetti with Chicken Meatballs

Serves 4–6

500 g (1 lb 2 oz) ground (minced) chicken

60 g (2¼ oz) freshly grated parmesan cheese

160 g (5½ oz/2 cups) fresh white breadcrumbs

2 garlic cloves, crushed

1 egg

1 tablespoon chopped flat-leaf (Italian) parsley

1 tablespoon chopped sage

60 ml (2 fl oz/¼ cup) vegetable oil

500 g (1 lb 2 oz) spaghetti

1 handful chopped oregano, to serve

TOMATO SAUCE

1 tablespoon olive oil

1 onion, finely chopped

2 kg (4 lb 8 oz) ripe tomatoes, chopped

2 bay leaves

2 large handfuls basil leaves

1 teaspoon coarsely ground black pepper

1   In a large bowl, mix the chicken, parmesan cheese, breadcrumbs, garlic, egg and herbs. Season to taste. Shape tablespoonsful of the mixture into small balls and refrigerate for about 30 minutes, to firm.

2   Heat the oil in a shallow frying pan and fry the balls, in batches, until golden brown. Turn them often by gently shaking the pan. Drain on paper towels.

3 To make the tomato sauce, heat the oil in a large saucepan. Add the onion and fry for about 1–2 minutes, until softened. Add the tomato and bay leaves. Cover and bring to the boil, stirring occasionally. Reduce the heat to low, partially cover and cook for 50–60 minutes.

4 Add the meatballs to the sauce, along with the basil leaves and freshly ground black pepper and simmer, uncovered, for 10–15 minutes.

5 Meanwhile, cook the spaghetti in a saucepan of boiling salted water until *al dente*. Drain and return to the pan to keep warm. Add some sauce to the pasta and toss to combine. Serve the pasta in individual bowls with sauce and meatballs, sprinkled with chopped oregano.

Chicken Carbonara

Serves 4

500 g (1 lb 2 oz) tomato fettucine
600 g (1 lb 5 oz) chicken tenderloins (breast underfillets)
40 g (1½ oz) butter
3 eggs
300 ml (10½ fl oz) pouring cream
50 g (1¾ oz/½ cup) grated parmesan cheese
shaved parmesan cheese, to serve

1 Cook the fettucine in a saucepan of boiling salted water until *al dente*. Drain and return to the pan to keep warm.

2 Trim and slice the tenderloins in half on the diagonal. Melt the butter in a frying pan and cook the chicken for 4–5 minutes, or until browned. Lightly beat the eggs and cream together and stir in the grated parmesan cheese. Season with salt to taste and stir through the chicken.

3 Add the fettucine to the chicken and cream mixture in the frying pan. Reduce the heat and cook, stirring constantly, for 10–15 seconds, or until the sauce is slightly thickened. Do not keep on the heat too long or the eggs will set and scramble. Season with black pepper and serve, garnished with parmesan cheese.

Saffron fettucine can be purchased from delicatessens or pasta shops, and is a good substitute for tomato fettucine.

Penne with Sautéed Chicken, Asparagus and Goat's Cheese

Serves 4

500 g (1 lb 2 oz) penne
350 g (12 oz) asparagus spears
1 tablespoon olive oil
2 chicken breast fillets, cut into small cubes
1 tablespoon finely chopped thyme
250 ml (9 fl oz/1 cup) chicken stock
80 ml (2³/4 fl oz/¹/3 cup) balsamic vinegar
150 g (5¹/2 oz) goat's cheese, crumbled

1 Cook the penne in a saucepan of boiling salted water until *al dente*. Drain and return to the pan to keep warm.

2 Remove the woody ends from the asparagus and cut into short lengths. Cook in a saucepan of boiling water for 3 minutes, or until just tender.

3 Heat the oil in a frying pan over high heat. Add the chicken and cook in batches, stirring occasionally, for 5 minutes, or until browned. Return all the chicken to the pan. Add the thyme and cook for 1 minute. Add the stock and vinegar and bring to the boil. Reduce the heat and simmer, stirring, for 3–4 minutes, or until the sauce has reduced slightly, then add the asparagus. Toss the pasta with the chicken and sprinkle with the cheese. Season and serve immediately.

Chicken Agnolotti

Serves 4

PASTA

250 g (9 oz/2 cups) plain (all-purpose) flour

3 eggs

1 tablespoon olive oil

1 egg yolk, extra

FILLING

125 g ($4^1/2$ oz) ground (minced) chicken

75 g ($2^1/2$ oz) ricotta cheese

60 g ($2^1/4$ oz) chicken livers, trimmed and chopped

30 g (1 oz) prosciutto, chopped

1 salami slice, chopped

40 g ($1^1/2$ oz) grated parmesan cheese

1 egg, beaten

1 small handful chopped flat-leaf (Italian) parsley

1 garlic clove, crushed

$1/4$ teaspoon mixed spice

TOMATO SAUCE

2 tablespoons olive oil

1 onion, finely chopped

2 garlic cloves, crushed

850 g (1 lb 14 oz) tinned crushed tomatoes

15 g ($1/2$ oz/$1/4$ cup) chopped basil

$1/2$ teaspoon mixed herbs

1   To make the pasta, sift the flour and a pinch of salt onto a board. Make a well in the centre of the flour. In a bowl, whisk together the

eggs, oil and 1 tablespoon water. Add the egg mixture gradually to the flour, working in with your hands until the mixture forms a ball. Knead on a lightly floured surface for 5 minutes, or until smooth and elastic. Place the dough in a lightly oiled bowl and cover with plastic wrap. Allow to stand for 30 minutes.

2 To make the filling, place the chicken, cheese, liver, prosciutto, salami, parmesan cheese, egg, parsley, garlic, mixed spice and salt and ground black pepper in a food processor. Process until finely chopped. Set aside.

3 To make the tomato sauce, heat the oil in a saucepan. Add the onion and garlic and stir over low heat until the onion is tender. Increase the heat, add the undrained, crushed tomatoes, basil, herbs, and salt and pepper. Stir to combine, then bring to the boil. Reduce the heat and simmer for 15 minutes. Remove from the heat.

4 Roll out half the pasta dough until 1 mm (¹/₁₆ in) thick. Cut with a knife or fluted pastry cutter into 10 cm (4 in) strips. Place teaspoons of filling at 5 cm (2 in) intervals down one side of each strip. Whisk together the extra egg yolk and 60 ml (2 fl oz/¼ cup) water. Brush along one side of the dough and between the filling. Fold the dough over the filling to meet the other side. Repeat with the remaining filling and dough.

5 Press the edges of the dough together firmly to seal. Cut between the mounds of filling with a knife or a fluted pastry cutter.

6 Cook the ravioli in batches in a saucepan of boiling salted water until *al dente*. Reheat the tomato sauce in a large saucepan. Add the cooked ravioli and toss well. Simmer, stirring, for 5 minutes. Serve immediately.

Pesto Chicken Penne

Serves 4

250 g (9 oz) penne
1 small barbecued chicken
125 g (4^1/$_2$ oz/1 cup) walnuts
4 bacon slices
250 g (9 oz) cherry tomatoes, halved
60 g (2^1/$_4$ oz) pitted and sliced olives
125 g (4^1/$_2$ oz/^{1}/$_2$ cup) pesto sauce
30 g (1 oz/^{1}/$_2$ cup) finely shredded basil
shaved parmesan cheese, to serve

1   Cook the penne in a saucepan of boiling salted water until *al dente*.
    Drain well and return to the pan to keep warm.

2   Meanwhile, discard the skin of the chicken. Remove the meat from
    the chicken, cut it into bite-sized pieces and put in a large bowl.

3   Toast the walnuts for 2–3 minutes under a hot grill (broiler), allow to
    cool and then chop roughly.

4   Remove the rind from the bacon slices and grill (broil) the bacon for
    3–4 minutes, or until crisp. Allow to cool, then chop into small pieces.
    Add the nuts, bacon, cherry tomatoes and olives to the chicken.

5   Add the pasta to the chicken mixture, along with the pesto sauce
    and basil. Toss until well combined. Serve at room temperature, with
    parmesan shavings.

Chicken Ravioli with Buttered Sage Sauce

Serves 4

500 g (1 lb 2 oz) chicken ravioli
60 g (2 1/4 oz) butter
4 spring onions (scallions), chopped
2 tablespoons sage, chopped
50 g (1 3/4 oz/ 1/2 cup) freshly grated parmesan cheese, to serve

1   Cook the ravioli in a saucepan of boiling salted water until *al dente*. Drain and return to the pan to keep warm.

2   While the ravioli is cooking, melt the butter in a heavy-based frying pan. Add the spring onion and sage and stir for 2 minutes. Season with salt and pepper.

3   Add the sauce to the pasta and toss well. Divide among four serving bowls and sprinkle with parmesan cheese. Serve immediately.

Ricotta-stuffed Conchiglie with Chicken Sauce

Serves 4

500 g (1 lb 2 oz) conchiglie
2 tablespoons olive oil
1 onion, chopped
1 garlic clove, crushed
60 g (2¼ oz) prosciutto, sliced
125 g (4½ oz) mushrooms, chopped
250 g (9 oz) ground (minced) chicken
2 tablespoons tomato paste (concentrated purée)
425 g (15 oz) tinned crushed tomatoes
125 ml (4 fl oz/½ cup) dry white wine
1 teaspoon dried oregano
250 g (9 oz) ricotta cheese
220 g (7¾ oz) mozzarella cheese, grated
1 teaspoon chopped chives
1 small handful chopped flat-leaf (Italian) parsley
60 g (2¼ oz) grated parmesan cheese

1 Cook the conchiglie in a saucepan of boiling salted water until *al dente*. Drain and return to the pan to keep warm.

2 Heat the oil in a frying pan. Add the onion and garlic and stir over low heat until the onion is tender. Add the prosciutto and stir for 1 minute. Add the mushrooms and cook for 2 minutes. Add the chicken and brown well, breaking up any lumps with a fork as it cooks.

3 Stir in the tomato paste, tomatoes, wine and oregano and season to taste. Bring to the boil, reduce the heat and simmer for 20 minutes.

4 Preheat the oven to 180°C (350°F/Gas 4). Combine the ricotta, mozzarella, chives, parsley and half the parmesan. Spoon a little into each shell. Spoon some of the chicken sauce into the base of a casserole dish. Arrange the conchiglie on top. Spread the remaining sauce over the top and sprinkle with the remaining parmesan. Bake 25–30 minutes, or until golden.

Lasagnette with Spicy Chicken Meatballs

Serves 4

750 g (1 lb 10 oz) ground (minced) chicken
1 handful chopped coriander (cilantro) leaves
1 1/2 tablespoons red curry paste
2 tablespoons oil
1 red onion, finely chopped
3 garlic cloves, crushed
875 ml (30 fl oz oz/3 1/2 cups) tomato pasta sauce
2 teaspoons soft brown sugar
350 g (12 oz) lasagnette

1 Line a baking tray with baking paper. Combine the chicken, coriander and 1 tablespoon of the curry paste in a bowl. Roll heaped tablespoons of the mixture into balls and put on the tray — you should get about 20 balls. Refrigerate until ready to use.

2 Heat the oil in a large deep frying pan. Cook the onion and garlic over medium heat for 2–3 minutes, or until softened. Add the remaining curry paste. Cook, stirring, for 1 minute, or until fragrant. Add the pasta sauce and sugar and stir well. Reduce the heat and add the meatballs. Cook, turning halfway through, for 10 minutes, or until the meatballs are cooked through.

3 Meanwhile, cook the pasta in a saucepan of boiling salted water until *al dente*. Drain and divide among four serving bowls. Top with the sauce and meatballs.

Creamy Rigatoni with Chicken and Sun-dried Tomato Sauce

Serves 4–6

500 g (1 lb 2 oz) rigatoni
1 tablespoon olive oil
4 chicken breast fillets, thinly sliced
4 ripe tomatoes, diced
150 g (5$^{1}/_{2}$ oz) sun-dried tomatoes in oil, thinly sliced
2 tablespoons sun-dried tomato paste (concentrated purée)
1 handful small basil leaves
300 ml (10$^{1}/_{2}$ fl oz) pouring cream
200 ml (7 fl oz) chicken stock

1 Cook the rigatoni in a saucepan of boiling salted water until *al dente*. Drain and return to the pan to keep warm.

2 Meanwhile, heat the oil in a deep frying pan and cook the chicken over high heat for 4 minutes each side, or until browned and cooked through. Remove from the pan and keep warm.

3 Return the pan to the heat and add the tomato, sun-dried tomato, sun-dried tomato paste and half the basil leaves. Cook over medium heat for 5 minutes, or until the tomato starts to soften. Stir in the cream and chicken stock. Bring to the boil, stirring constantly.

4 Reduce the heat and return the chicken to the pan. Add the rigatoni and season with pepper. Heat gently until the chicken and pasta are warmed through. Top with the remaining basil leaves.

Chicken Ravioli with Tomato Sauce

Serves 4

TOMATO SAUCE
1 teaspoon olive oil
1 large onion, chopped
2 garlic cloves, crushed
90 g (3 oz/^{1}/3 cup) tomato paste (concentrated purée)
60 ml (2 fl oz/^{1}/4 cup) red wine
170 ml (5^1/2 fl oz/^{2}/3 cup) chicken stock
2 tomatoes, chopped
1 small handful chopped basil

RAVIOLI
200 g (7 oz) ground (minced) chicken
1 small handful chopped basil
25 g (1 oz/^{1}/4 cup) grated parmesan cheese
3 spring onions (scallions), finely chopped
50 g (1^3/4 oz) ricotta cheese
250 g (9 oz) packet round won ton or gow gee wrappers

1 To make the tomato sauce, heat the oil in a saucepan. Cook the onion
and garlic for 2–3 minutes, then stir in the tomato paste, wine, stock
and tomato. Simmer for 20 minutes. Stir in the basil.

2 To make the ravioli, combine the chicken, basil, parmesan, spring
onion and ricotta. Lay 24 of the wrappers on a flat surface and brush
with a little water. Place 1 teaspoon of the mixture onto the centre of
each wrapper. Place another wrapper on top. Press the edges together.

3 Bring a saucepan of water to the boil. Cook the ravioli, in batches, for
2–3 minutes, or until *al dente*. Drain. Serve with the tomato sauce.

Creamy Chicken and Peppercorn Pappardelle

Serves 4

2 chicken breast fillets
30 g (1 oz) butter
1 onion, halved and thinly sliced
2 tablespoons drained green peppercorns, slightly crushed
125 ml (4 fl oz/$1/2$ cup) white wine
300 ml ($10^1/2$ fl oz) pouring cream
400 g (14 oz) pappardelle
80 g ($2^3/4$ oz/$1/3$ cup) sour cream (optional), to serve
1 handful chopped fresh chives, to garnish

1 Cut the chicken fillets in half so that you have four flat fillets and season. Melt the butter in a frying pan over medium heat. Add the chicken and cook for 3 minutes each side, or until cooked through. Remove from the pan, cut into slices and keep warm.

2 Add the onion and peppercorns to the frying pan and cook for 3 minutes, or until the onion has softened slightly. Add the wine and cook for 1 minute, or until reduced by half. Stir in the cream and cook for 4–5 minutes, or until thickened slightly, then season.

3 Meanwhile, cook the pasta in a saucepan of boiling salted water until *al dente*, then drain. Mix together the pasta, chicken and any juices and the cream sauce. Divide the pasta among serving bowls, top with a dollop of sour cream and sprinkle with chives.

Brandy Chicken Fettucine

Serves 4–6

10 g (1/4 oz) porcini mushrooms
2 tablespoons olive oil
2 garlic cloves, crushed
200 g (7 oz) button mushrooms, sliced
125 g (41/2 oz) prosciutto, chopped
375 g (13 oz) fettucine
60 ml (2 fl oz/1/4 cup) brandy
250 ml (9 fl oz/1 cup) pouring cream
1 barbecued chicken, skin removed, meat shredded
155 g (51/2 oz/1 cup) frozen peas
2 large handfuls finely chopped flat-leaf (Italian) parsley

1   Put the porcini mushrooms in a bowl and cover with boiling water. Set aside for 10 minutes, then drain, squeeze dry and chop.

2   Heat the oil in a large, heavy-based frying pan. Add the crushed garlic and cook, stirring, for 1 minute over low heat. Add the button and porcini mushrooms, along with the prosciutto, and cook over low heat, stirring often, for 5 minutes.

3   Meanwhile, cook the pasta in a saucepan of boiling salted water until *al dente*. Drain and return to the pan to keep warm.

4   Add the brandy and cream to the mushroom mixture. Cook, stirring, over low heat for 2 minutes. Add the chicken, peas and parsley. Cook, stirring, for 4–5 minutes, until heated through. Add the chicken mixture to the pasta and serve immediately.

Chicken Ravioli with Lime Balsamic Dressing

Serves 4

250 g (9 oz) ground (minced) chicken
1 egg, lightly beaten
1 teaspoon finely grated orange zest
50 g (1³/4 oz/¹/2 cup) freshly grated parmesan cheese
1 tablespoon finely shredded basil
275 g (9³/4 oz) won ton wrappers
2 tablespoons lime juice
2 tablespoons balsamic vinegar
¹/2 teaspoon honey
1 tablespoon oil

1 Combine the chicken, egg, orange zest, parmesan and basil in a bowl. Place a heaped tablespoon of chicken mixture in the centre of a won ton wrapper, lightly brush the edges with water and top with another wrapper. Press the edges together. Repeat with remaining filling and wrappers.

2 Cook the chicken ravioli in a saucepan of boiling salted water for 5 minutes, or until *al dente*. Drain and return to the pan to keep warm.

3 Meanwhile, combine the lime juice, balsamic vinegar, honey and oil in a small jug and whisk to combine. Serve the ravioli drizzled with the dressing.

Chicken Tortellini with Tomato Sauce

Serves 4

PASTA
250 g (9 oz/2 cups) plain (all-purpose) flour
3 eggs
1 tablespoon olive oil

FILLING
20 g (1 oz) butter
80 g (2³/4 oz) chicken breast fillet, cubed
2 slices pancetta, chopped
50 g (1³/4 oz/¹/2 cup) grated parmesan cheese
¹/2 teaspoon nutmeg
1 egg, lightly beaten

TOMATO SAUCE
80 ml (2³/4 fl oz/¹/3 cup) olive oil
1.5 kg (3 lb 5 oz) ripe tomatoes, peeled and chopped
1 handful chopped oregano
50 g (1³/4 oz/¹/2 cup) grated parmesan cheese

100 g (3¹/2 oz) bocconcini (fresh baby mozzarella cheese), sliced, to serve

1   To make the pasta, sift the flour and a pinch of salt into a bowl and make a well in the centre. In a jug, whisk together the eggs, oil and 1 tablespoon of water. Add the egg mixture gradually to the flour, mixing to a firm dough. Gather together into a ball.

2   Knead on a lightly floured surface for 5 minutes, or until the dough is smooth and elastic. Place in a lightly oiled bowl, cover with plastic wrap and leave for 30 minutes.

3   To make the filling, heat the butter in a frying pan over medium heat. Add the chicken and cook until golden brown, then drain. Process the chicken and pancetta in a food processor until finely chopped. Transfer to a bowl and add the cheese, nutmeg, egg and salt and pepper. Set aside.

4   Roll out the dough very thinly on a lightly floured surface. Using a floured cutter, cut into 5 cm (2 in) rounds. Spoon about ½ teaspoon of filling into the centre of each round. Fold the rounds in half to form semicircles, pressing the edges together firmly. Wrap each semicircle around your finger to form a ring and then press the ends of the dough together firmly.

5   To make the tomato sauce, cook the oil, tomato and oregano in a frying pan over high heat for 10 minutes. Stir in the parmesan, then set aside.

6   Cook the tortellini in two batches in a saucepan of boiling salted water for about 6 minutes each batch, or until *al dente*. Drain and return to the pan to keep warm. Reheat the tomato sauce, add to the tortellini and toss to combine. Divide the tortellini among individual bowls, top with the bocconcini and allow the cheese to melt a little before serving.

To peel fresh tomatoes, score a cross in the base of the tomato, put in a bowl of boiling water for 1 minute, then plunge into cold water. The skin will peel away from the cross.

Chicken with Lemon, Parsley and Orecchiette

Serves 4

375 g (13 oz) orecchiette
1 tablespoon oil
60 g (2¼ oz) butter
4 small chicken breast fillets
80 ml (2¾ fl oz/⅓ cup) lemon juice
2 large handfuls finely chopped flat-leaf (Italian) parsley
lemon slices, to garnish

1 Cook the orecchiette in a saucepan of boiling salted water until *al dente*. Drain and return to the pan to keep warm.

2 Meanwhile, heat the oil and half the butter in a large heavy-based frying pan. Add the chicken fillets and cook for 2 minutes each side, then set aside. Add the lemon juice, parsley and the remaining butter to the pan. Stir to combine and return the fillets to the pan. Cook over low heat for 3–4 minutes, turning once, or until cooked through. Season with salt and freshly ground black pepper.

3 Serve the pasta topped with a chicken fillet and sauce. Garnish with lemon slices.

Spaghetti with Chicken Bolognese

serves 4

2 tablespoons olive oil

2 leeks, thinly sliced

1 red capsicum (pepper), diced

2 garlic cloves, crushed

500 g (1 lb 2 oz) ground (minced) chicken

500 ml (17 fl oz/2 cups) tomato pasta sauce

1 tablespoon chopped thyme

1 tablespoon chopped rosemary

40 g (1¹/2 oz) pitted and chopped black olives

400 g (14 oz) spaghetti

125 g (4¹/2 oz) feta cheese, crumbled

1 Heat the oil in a large heavy-based frying pan. Add the leek, capsicum and garlic and cook over medium–high heat for 2 minutes, or until lightly browned.

2 Add the chicken and cook, stirring occasionally, over high heat for 3 minutes, or until browned, breaking up any lumps with a fork as it cooks.

3 Add the tomato pasta sauce, thyme and rosemary and bring to the boil. Reduce the heat and simmer for 5 minutes, or until the sauce has reduced and thickened. Add the olives and stir to combine. Season to taste.

4 Cook the spaghetti in a saucepan of boiling salted water until *al dente*. Drain. Divide the spaghetti among serving plates and pour the bolognese over the top. Sprinkle with feta and serve immediately.

Low-fat Chicken and Vegetable Lasagne

Serves 8

500 g (1 lb 2 oz) chicken breast fillets
cooking oil spray
2 garlic cloves, crushed
1 onion, chopped
2 zucchini (courgettes), chopped
2 celery stalks, chopped
2 carrots, chopped
300 g (10 1/2 oz) pumpkin (winter squash), diced
800 g (1 lb 12 oz) tinned crushed tomatoes
2 sprigs thyme
2 bay leaves
125 ml (4 fl oz/1/2 cup) white wine
2 tablespoons tomato paste (concentrated purée)
1 handful chopped basil
500 g (1 lb 2 oz) English spinach
500 g (1 lb 2 oz) cottage cheese
450 g (1 lb) ricotta cheese
60 ml (2 fl oz/1/4 cup) low-fat milk
1/2 teaspoon ground nutmeg
35 g (1 1/4 oz/1/3 cup) grated parmesan cheese
300 g (10 1/2 oz) lasagne sheets

1 Preheat the oven to 180°C (350°F/Gas 4). Trim any excess fat from the chicken breasts, then finely grind (mince) in a food processor.

2 Heat a large deep non-stick frying pan over medium heat. Spray lightly with oil and cook the chicken in batches until browned. Remove and set aside.

3 Add the garlic and onion to the pan and cook until softened. Return the chicken to the pan and add the zucchini, celery, carrot, pumpkin, tomato, thyme, bay leaves, wine and tomato paste. Simmer, covered, for 20 minutes. Remove the bay leaves and thyme, stir in the basil and set aside.

4 Shred the spinach and set aside. Mix the cottage cheese, ricotta, skim milk, nutmeg and half the parmesan.

5 Spoon a little of the tomato mixture over the base of a casserole dish and top with a single layer of pasta. Top with half the remaining tomato mixture, then the spinach and spoon over half the cottage cheese mixture. Continue with another layer of pasta, the remaining tomato and another layer of pasta. Spread the remaining cottage cheese mixture on top and sprinkle with parmesan. Bake for 40–50 minutes, or until golden.

Penne with Chicken and Mushrooms

Serves 4

30 g (1 oz) butter
1 tablespoon olive oil
1 onion, sliced
1 garlic clove, crushed
60 g (2¼ oz) prosciutto, chopped
250 g (9 oz) chicken thigh fillets, trimmed and sliced
125 g (4½ oz) mushrooms, sliced
1 tomato, peeled, halved and sliced
1 tablespoon tomato paste (concentrated purée)
125 ml (4 fl oz/½ cup) white wine
250 ml (9 fl oz/1 cup) pouring cream
500 g (1 lb 2 oz) penne
40 g (1½ oz) grated parmesan cheese, to serve

1 Heat the butter and oil in a large frying pan. Add the onion and garlic and stir over low heat until the onion is tender. Add the prosciutto and fry until crisp.

2 Add the chicken and cook over medium heat for 3 minutes. Add the mushrooms and cook for 2 minutes. Stir in the tomato and tomato paste and then the wine. Bring to the boil. Reduce the heat and simmer until reduced by half.

3 Stir in the cream and season. Bring to the boil. Reduce the heat and simmer until the sauce begins to thicken.

4 Meanwhile, cook the penne in a saucepan of boiling salted water until *al dente*. Drain and return to the pan to keep warm. Add the sauce and toss. Serve sprinkled with parmesan.

Chicken, Broccoli and Macaroni Bake

Serves 6–8

300 g (10¹/2 oz) macaroni
425 g (14 oz) tinned cream of mushroom soup
2 eggs
185 g (6¹/2 oz/³/4 cup) mayonnaise
1 tablespoon dijon mustard
200 g (7 oz/1²/3 cups) grated cheddar cheese
600 g (1 lb 5 oz) chicken breast fillets, thinly sliced
400 g (14 oz) frozen broccoli pieces, thawed
40 g (1¹/4 oz/¹/2 cup) fresh breadcrumbs

1 Preheat the oven to 180°C (350°F/Gas 4). Cook the macaroni in a saucepan of boiling salted water until *al dente*. Drain and return to the pan to keep warm. Combine the soup, eggs, mayonnaise, mustard and half the cheese in a bowl.

2 Heat a lightly greased non-stick frying pan over medium heat. Add the chicken and cook for 5–6 minutes, or until cooked through. Season with salt and pepper, then set aside to cool.

3 Add the chicken and broccoli to the pasta. Pour the soup mixture over the top and stir until well combined. Transfer the mixture to a 3 litre (104 fl oz/12 cup) ovenproof dish. Sprinkle with the combined breadcrumbs and remaining cheese. Bake for 20 minutes, or until golden brown.

Tagliatelle with Octopus Smoked Salmon ⅝

Pasta with seafood

elle Spaghetti Marinara Seafood Cannelloni

Tagliatelle with Octopus

Serves 4

500 g (1 lb 2 oz) tagliatelle
2 tablespoons olive oil
1 onion, sliced
1 garlic clove, crushed
425 g (14 oz) tinned crushed tomatoes
125 ml (4 fl oz/¹/₂ cup) dry white wine
chilli sauce, to taste
1 tablespoon chopped basil
1 kg (2 lb 4 oz) baby octopus, cleaned and halved

1 Cook the tagliatelle in a saucepan of boiling salted water until *al dente*. Drain and return to the pan to keep warm.

2 Meanwhile, heat the oil in a large frying pan. Add the onion and garlic and stir over low heat until the onion is tender. Add the crushed tomatoes, wine, chilli sauce, basil and season with salt and pepper. Bring to the boil. Reduce the heat and simmer for 10 minutes.

3 Add the octopus to the sauce. Simmer for 5–10 minutes or until the octopus is tender. Pour over the pasta and serve immediately.

To clean octopus, using a small knife, cut and remove the gut by slicing open the head and removing the gut. Pick up the body and use your index finger to push the beak up. Remove the beak. Wash the octopus thoroughly. Cut the sac into two pieces.

Smoked Salmon Pappardelle

Serves 4

500 g (1 lb 2 oz) pappardelle
1 tablespoon olive oil
4 spring onions (scallions), finely chopped
180 g (6¹/₂ oz) button mushrooms, sliced
250 ml (9 fl oz/1 cup) dry white wine
300 ml (10¹/₂ fl oz) pouring cream
1 tablespoon finely chopped dill
1 tablespoon lemon juice
90 g (3¹/₄ oz) parmesan cheese, grated
200 g (7 oz) smoked salmon, cut into strips
shaved parmesan cheese and lemon wedges, to serve

1 Cook the pappardelle in a saucepan of boiling salted water until *al dente*. Drain and return to the pan to keep warm.

2 Meanwhile, heat the oil in a small saucepan. Add the spring onion and mushrooms and cook over medium heat for 1–2 minutes, or until soft. Add the wine and cream and bring to the boil, then reduce the heat and simmer for 1 minute.

3 Pour the mushroom sauce over the pasta and stir through the dill and lemon juice. Add the parmesan and stir until warmed through. Remove from the heat and stir in the smoked salmon. Season with pepper and serve with parmesan shavings and lemon wedges.

Angel Hair Pasta with Garlic, Scallops and Rocket

Serves 4

20 large scallops with roe
250 g (9 oz) angel hair pasta
150 ml (5 fl oz) extra virgin olive oil
2 garlic cloves, finely chopped
60 ml (2 fl oz/1/4 cup) white wine
1 tablespoon lemon juice
100 g (3 1/2 oz) baby rocket (arugula) leaves
30 g (1 oz/1/2 cup) chopped coriander (cilantro) leaves

1 Pull or trim any veins, membrane or hard white muscle from the scallops. Pat the scallops dry with paper towels. Cook the pasta in a saucepan of boiling salted water until *al dente*. Drain and transfer to a bowl. Toss with 1 tablespoon of the oil.

2 Meanwhile, heat 1 tablespoon oil in a frying pan. Add the garlic and cook for a few seconds, or until fragrant. Do not brown. Add the wine and lemon juice, and remove from the heat.

3 Heat a chargrill pan or barbecue grill plate over high heat and brush with a little oil. Season the scallops with salt and pepper and cook for 1 minute each side, or until just cooked. Gently reheat the garlic mixture, add the rocket and stir over medium heat for 1–2 minutes, or until wilted. Toss through the pasta and mix well. Add the remaining oil and half the coriander and mix well. Divide the pasta among four bowls, arrange the scallops over the top and garnish with the remaining coriander.

Spaghetti with Tuna, Basil and Capers

Serves 4

500 g (1 lb 2 oz) spaghetti
1 tablespoon extra virgin olive oil
2 garlic cloves, crushed
250 g (9 oz) tinned tuna in brine, drained and broken into chunks
4 handfuls basil leaves, torn
4 vine-ripened tomatoes, roughly chopped
2 tablespoons capers, roughly chopped
90 g (3 1/4 oz) parmesan cheese, grated

1 Cook the pasta in a saucepan of boiling salted water until *al dente*. Drain and return to the pan to keep warm.

2 Meanwhile, heat the oil in a small saucepan. Add the garlic and tuna and cook over medium heat for 1 minute, or until the garlic is fragrant and the tuna is warmed through.

3 Add the tuna mixture, basil, tomato, capers and parmesan to the spaghetti and mix well. Season and serve immediately.

Spaghetti Marinara

Serves 6

12 fresh mussels

TOMATO SAUCE
2 tablespoons olive oil
1 onion, finely diced
1 carrot, sliced
1 red chilli, seeded and chopped
2 garlic cloves, crushed
425 g (14 oz) tinned crushed tomatoes
125 ml (4 fl oz/$1/2$ cup) white wine
1 teaspoon sugar
pinch of cayenne pepper

60 ml (2 fl oz/$1/4$ cup) white wine
60 ml (2 fl oz/$1/4$ cup) fish stock
1 garlic clove, crushed
375 g (13 oz) spaghetti
30 g (1 oz) butter
125 g ($4^1/2$ oz) small calamari tubes, sliced
125 g ($4^1/2$ oz) boneless white fish fillets, cut into cubes
200 g (7 oz) raw prawns (shrimp), shelled and deveined
1 large handful flat-leaf (Italian) parsley, chopped
200 g (7 oz) tinned clams, drained

1. Remove the beards from the mussels and scrub away any grit. Discard any opened or damaged mussels.

2. To make the tomato sauce, heat the oil in a frying pan, add the onion and carrot and stir over medium heat for about 10 minutes, or until the vegetables are lightly browned. Add the chilli, garlic, tomato, white wine, sugar and cayenne pepper and simmer for 30 minutes, stirring occasionally.

3. Meanwhile, heat the wine with the stock and garlic in a large saucepan and add the unopened mussels. Cover the pan and shake it over high heat for 3–5 minutes. After 3 minutes, start removing any opened mussels and set them aside. After 5 minutes discard any unopened mussels and reserve the wine mixture.

4. Cook the pasta in a saucepan of boiling salted water until *al dente*. Drain and return to the pan to keep warm.

5. Meanwhile, melt the butter in a frying pan. Add the calamari rings, fish and prawns and stir-fry for 2 minutes. Set aside. Add the reserved wine mixture, mussels, calamari, fish, prawns, parsley and clams to the tomato sauce and reheat gently. Gently combine the sauce with the pasta and serve immediately.

Salmon with Pappardelle and Saffron Cream Sauce

Serves 4

500 g (1 lb 2 oz) pappardelle
50 g (1³/4 oz) butter
4 garlic cloves, crushed
150 g (5¹/2 oz) oyster mushrooms
800 g (1 lb 12 oz) raw prawns (shrimp), peeled and deveined
2 x 400 g (14 oz) salmon fillets, skin removed, cut into small cubes
250 ml (9 fl oz/1 cup) white wine
250 ml (9 fl oz/1 cup) fish stock
¹/4 teaspoon saffron threads
400 g (14 oz) crème fraîche
125 g (4¹/2 oz) sugar snap peas

1 Cook the pappardelle in a saucepan of boiling salted water until *al dente*. Drain and return to the pan to keep warm.

2 Meanwhile, melt the butter in a large deep frying pan, add the garlic and oyster mushrooms and cook for 1 minute. Add the prawns and salmon and cook for 2–3 minutes, or until the prawns are cooked and the salmon starts to flake. Transfer to a bowl.

3 Pour the wine and stock into the pan and add the saffron. Bring to the boil, then reduce the heat and simmer rapidly for 5 minutes, or until reduced by half. Add the crème fraîche and sugar snap peas and stir. Bring to the boil, then reduce the heat and simmer, stirring occasionally, for 3–4 minutes, until the liquid has slightly thickened.

4 Return the seafood and any juices to the pan and stir over medium heat until warmed through. Serve over the pasta.

Spaghetti with Olive, Caper and Anchovy Sauce

Serves 6

375 g (13 oz) spaghetti
80 ml (2³/4 fl oz/¹/3 cup) olive oil
2 onions, finely chopped
3 garlic cloves, finely chopped
¹/2 teaspoon chilli flakes
6 large ripe tomatoes, diced
4 tablespoons capers in brine, rinsed, drained
7–8 anchovies in oil, drained, minced
150 g (5¹/2 oz) kalamata olives
3 tablespoons chopped flat-leaf (Italian) parsley

1 Cook the pasta in a saucepan of boiling salted water until *al dente*. Drain and return to the pan to keep warm.

2 Meanwhile, heat the oil in a saucepan. Add the onion and cook over medium heat for 5 minutes. Add the garlic and chilli flakes, and cook for 30 seconds, then add the tomato, capers and anchovies. Simmer over low heat for 5–10 minutes, or until thick and pulpy, then stir in the olives and parsley.

3 Stir the pasta through the sauce. Season and serve immediately.

Cajun Scallops with Conchiglie and Buttery Corn Sauce

Serves 4

350 g (11 oz) conchiglie

20 large scallops, without roe

2 tablespoons cajun spice mix

2 tablespoons corn oil

250 g (9 oz) butter

3 garlic cloves, crushed

400 g (14 oz) tinned corn kernels, drained

60 ml (2 fl oz/^{1}/4 cup) lime juice

4 tablespoons finely chopped coriander (cilantro) leaves

1 Cook the conchiglie in a saucepan of boiling salted water until *al dente*. Drain and return to the pan to keep warm.

2 Meanwhile, pat the scallops dry with paper towels and lightly coat in the spice mix. Heat the oil in a large frying pan and cook the scallops for 1 minute each side over high heat (ensuring they are well spaced). Remove from the pan, cover and keep warm.

3 Reduce the heat to medium, add the butter and cook for 4 minutes, or until foaming and golden brown. Remove from the heat and add the garlic, corn and lime juice. Gently toss the corn mixture through the pasta with 2 tablespoons of the coriander and season well. Divide among four serving plates, top with the scallops, drizzle with any juices and sprinkle with the remaining coriander.

Orecchiette with Anchovies, Broccoli and Basil

serves 4–6

600 g (1 lb 5 oz) broccoli, cut into florets
500 g (1 lb 2 oz) orecchiette
1 tablespoon olive oil
4 garlic cloves, finely chopped
8 anchovy fillets, roughly chopped
250 ml (9 fl oz/1 cup) pouring cream
2 large handfuls basil, torn
2 teaspoons finely grated lemon zest
100 g (3½ oz) parmesan cheese, grated

1 Blanch the broccoli in a large saucepan of boiling salted water for 3–4 minutes. Remove and plunge into chilled water. Drain well.

2 Cook the orecchiette in a saucepan of boiling salted water until *al dente*. Drain and return to the pan to keep warm, reserving 2 tablespoons of the cooking water.

3 Meanwhile, heat the oil in a frying pan over medium heat. Add the garlic and anchovies and cook for 1–2 minutes, or until the garlic begins to turn golden. Add the broccoli and cook for a further 5 minutes. Add the cream and half the basil and cook for 10 minutes, or until the cream has slightly thickened and the broccoli is tender.

4 Purée half the mixture in a food processor until nearly smooth, then return to the pan with the lemon zest, half the parmesan and 2 tablespoons of the reserved water. Stir well, then season. Add the pasta and remaining basil, and toss until combined. Sprinkle with the remaining parmesan and serve.

Seafood Cannelloni

Serves 6

1 onion, sliced
1 carrot, sliced
1 celery stalk, cut in half
1 bouquet garni
250 ml (9 fl oz/1 cup) white wine
4 whole black peppercorns
300 g (10½ oz) scallops
500 g (1 lb 2 oz) raw prawns (shrimp)
300 g (10½ oz) skinless fish fillets (such as flathead, flake, hake,
    ling or cod), boned and chopped
60 g (2¼ oz) butter
1 onion, finely chopped
200 g (7 oz) button mushrooms, finely chopped
800 g (1 lb 12 oz) tinned crushed tomatoes
2 tablespoons chopped flat-leaf (Italian) parsley
2 tablespoons chopped basil
2 tablespoons pouring cream
15 cannelloni tubes
125 g (4½ oz) cheddar cheese, grated

BECHAMEL SAUCE
60 g (2¼ oz) butter
2 tablespoons plain (all-purpose) flour
750 ml (24 fl oz/3 cups) milk

1 Preheat the oven to 180°C (350°F/Gas 4). Combine the onion, carrot,
   celery, bouquet garni and 500 ml (17 fl oz/2 cups) water in a large

saucepan and bring to the boil. Reduce the heat and simmer for 15 minutes. Add the wine and peppercorns and simmer for 15 minutes. Strain, discard the vegetables and reserve the liquid.

2 Meanwhile, slice or pull off any vein, membrane or hard white muscle from the scallops, leaving any roe attached. Dice the scallops. Peel the prawns and gently pull out the dark vein from each prawn back, starting at the head end, and roughly dice the prawn meat. Cut the seafood small enough to fit in the cannelloni tubes.

3 Put the reserved liquid in a clean saucepan and bring to the boil. Add the seafood. Reduce the heat and simmer for 3 minutes, or until tender. Strain and reserve the liquid.

4 Melt the butter in a large frying pan. Add the onion and cook over medium heat until golden brown. Add the mushrooms and cook until tender. Add 60 ml (2 fl oz/$1/4$ cup) of the reserved liquid, the tomato and herbs and bring to the boil. Reduce the heat and simmer for 30 minutes, or until the sauce thickens slightly. Stir in the seafood and cream and season with salt and pepper to taste.

5 To make the béchamel sauce, melt the butter in a saucepan. Add the flour and stir for 1 minute, or until pale and foaming. Remove from the heat and gradually stir in the milk. Return to the heat and stir until the sauce comes to the boil and thickens.

6 Spoon the seafood mixture into the cannelloni tubes and place in a greased 3 litre (104 fl oz/12 cup) ovenproof dish. Pour the sauce over the top and sprinkle with the grated cheese. Bake for 40 minutes, or until the cannelloni tubes are tender.

Fettucine with Balsamic-Seared Tuna

serves 4–6

4 x 200 g (7 oz) tuna steaks
170 ml (5^1/2 oz/^{2}/3 cup) balsamic vinegar
125 ml (4 fl oz/^{1}/2 cup) good-quality olive oil
1 lemon
1 garlic clove, finely chopped
1 red onion, finely chopped
2 tablespoons capers, rinsed and dried
1 handful flat-leaf (italian) parsley, finely chopped
500 g (1 lb 2 oz) fettucine

1 Place the tuna steaks in a non-metallic dish and cover with the balsamic vinegar. Turn to coat evenly and marinate for 10 minutes. Heat 2 tablespoons of the oil in a large frying pan over medium heat and cook the tuna for 2–3 minutes each side. Remove from the pan, cut into small cubes and transfer to a bowl.

2 Finely grate the zest from the lemon to give ^{1}/2 teaspoon zest, then squeeze the lemon to give 60 ml (2 fl oz/^{1}/4 cup) juice. Wipe the frying pan clean, heat 2 tablespoons of the olive oil over medium heat, then add the garlic and cook for 30 seconds. Stir in the chopped onion and cook for 2 minutes. Add the lemon zest and capers and cook for 1 minute, then stir in the parsley and cook for 1 minute. Add the lemon juice and remaining oil and toss together. Season to taste.

3 Cook the fettucine in a saucepan of boiling salted water until *al dente*. Drain and return to the pan. Toss with the caper mixture. Divide the pasta among serving bowls and arrange the tuna pieces over the top.

Angel Hair Pasta with Creamy Garlic Prawns

Serves 4

2 tablespoons olive oil
16 raw prawns (shrimp), peeled and deveined
1 leek, chopped
6 garlic cloves, crushed
1/2 teaspoon dried chilli flakes
125 ml (4 fl oz/1/2 cup) dry white wine
200 ml (7 fl oz) pouring cream
250 g (9 oz) angel hair pasta
3 tablespoons chopped flat-leaf (Italian) parsley

1 Heat half the oil in a frying pan. Season the prawns with salt and pepper, add to the pan and cook over high heat for 2–3 minutes, or until cooked through. Remove from the pan, cover and keep warm.

2 Heat the remaining oil in the same pan, add the leek and cook, stirring, over medium heat for 2–3 minutes, or until softened. Add the garlic and chilli flakes and stir for 1 minute. Pour in the wine, reduce the heat and simmer for 4 minutes, or until reduced. Add the cream and simmer for 3 minutes, or until just thickened.

3 Meanwhile, cook the pasta in a saucepan of boiling salted water until *al dente*. Drain and return to the pan to keep warm. Stir the parsley into the sauce and season well. Add to the pasta and stir to coat. Divide the pasta among bowls and top with the prawns.

Spaghetti with Shellfish and White Wine Sauce

Serves 4

500 g (1 lb 2 oz) mussels

1 kg (2 lb 4 oz) clams

400 g (14 oz) spaghetti

2 tablespoons olive oil

4 French shallots, finely chopped

2 garlic cloves, crushed

250 ml (9 fl oz/1 cup) dry white wine

3 tablespoons chopped flat-leaf (Italian) parsley

1 Remove the beards from the mussels and scrub away any grit. Discard any opened or damaged mussels and clams. Wash them both thoroughly under cold running water. Cook the pasta in a saucepan of boiling salted water until *al dente*. Drain and return to the pan to keep warm.

2 Meanwhile, heat the oil in a large saucepan over medium heat. Cook the shallots for 4 minutes, or until softened. Add the garlic and cook for a further 1 minute. Pour in the wine, bring to the boil and cook for 2 minutes, or until reduced slightly. Add the clams and mussels, tossing to coat them in the liquid, then cover the pan. Cook, shaking the pan regularly, for about 3 minutes, or until the shells have opened. Discard any clams or mussels that do not open. Toss the clam mixture through the spaghetti and scatter with parsley.

Smoked Salmon Pappardelle in Champagne Sauce

Serves 4

375 g (12 oz) pappardelle
1 tablespoon olive oil
2 garlic cloves, crushed
125 ml (4 fl oz/^{1}/$_2$ cup) Champagne
250 ml (8 fl oz/1 cup) thick (double/heavy) cream
200 g (7 oz) smoked salmon, cut into thin strips
2 tablespoons small capers in brine, rinsed and dried
2 tablespoons chopped chives
2 tablespoons chopped dill

1 Cook the pasta in a saucepan of boiling salted water until *al dente*. Drain and return to the pan to keep warm. Heat the oil in a frying pan. Cook the garlic over medium heat for 30 seconds. Add the Champagne and cook for 2–3 minutes, or until reduced slightly. Add the cream and cook for 3–4 minutes, or until thickened.

2 Toss the sauce and remaining ingredients with the pasta and serve.

Salmon Pasta Soufflé

Serves 4

2 tablespoons grated parmesan cheese
60 g (2 1/4 oz) butter
1 small onion, finely chopped
2 tablespoons plain (all-purpose) flour
500 ml (17 fl oz/2 cups) milk
125 ml (4 fl oz/1/2 cup) chicken stock
3 eggs, separated
125 g (4 1/2 oz) small macaroni, cooked
210 g (7 oz) tinned salmon, drained and flaked
1 tablespoon chopped flat-leaf (Italian) parsley
grated zest of 1 lemon

1 Preheat the oven to 210°C (415°F/Gas 6–7). Brush a round 18 cm (7 in) soufflé dish with oil. Coat the base and sides with parmesan, shaking off the excess. Make a collar for the dish by cutting a piece of baking (parchment) paper a little longer than the circumference of the dish. Fold the paper in half lengthways and wrap around the outside of the dish so that it extends 5 cm (2 in) above the rim. Secure with string.

2 Heat the butter in a large saucepan and cook the onion over low heat until tender. Add the flour. Stir for 2 minutes or until lightly golden. Remove from heat and gradually stir in the milk and stock until smooth. Return to the heat and stir constantly until the mixture boils and thickens. Reduce the heat and simmer for 3 minutes. Add the egg yolks and whisk until smooth. Add the macaroni, salmon, parsley, lemon zest and some salt and pepper. Stir well and transfer to a bowl to cool.

3 Beat the egg whites in a small dry bowl until stiff peaks form. Using a metal spoon, fold gently into the salmon mixture. Spoon into the soufflé dish. Bake for 40–45 minutes or until well risen. Serve immediately.

 Hot soufflés should be served immediately as they will collapse very quickly after removal from the oven. The base mixture can be prepared, up to the end of Step 2, well in advance and refrigerated. Soften the mixture before folding in beaten egg whites. The whites should be folded into the mixture just before cooking.

Pappardelle with Fresh Salmon and Gremolata

Serves 4

30 g (1 oz/½ cup) chopped flat-leaf (Italian) parsley

3 teaspoons grated lemon zest

2 garlic cloves, finely chopped

400 g (14 oz) pappardelle

60 ml (2 fl oz/¼ cup) extra virgin olive oil

500 g (1 lb 2 oz) salmon fillet

2 teaspoons olive oil, extra

1   To make the gremolata, put the parsley, lemon zest and garlic in a bowl and mix together well. Cook the pasta in a saucepan of boiling salted water until *al dente*. Drain, transfer to a bowl, then add the olive oil and toss gently. Add the gremolata and toss again.

2   Remove the skin and any bones from the salmon. Heat the extra olive oil in a frying pan and cook the salmon over medium heat for 3–4 minutes, turning once during cooking. Take care not to overcook the fish. Flake the salmon into large pieces and toss through the pasta. Season to taste with salt and cracked black pepper and divide among four warm serving plates.

Seafood Lasagne

Serves 4

1 tablespoon olive oil
2 garlic cloves, crushed
1/4 teaspoon saffron threads
600 ml (21 fl oz) tomato pasta sauce
750 g (1 lb 10 oz) mixed raw seafood, cut into bite-sized pieces
   (you can use a prepared marinara mix)
4 fresh lasagne sheets, cut into twelve 10 x 16 cm (4 x 7 in) rectangles
120 g (4¹/4 oz) English spinach
185 g (6 oz/³/4 cup) mascarpone
90 g (3 oz/³/4 cup) grated parmesan cheese

1   Heat the oil in a large saucepan. Add the garlic, saffron and pasta sauce, reduce the heat and simmer for 8 minutes, or until thickened slightly. Add the seafood and cook for 2 minutes, or until cooked, then season. Remove from the heat.

2   Cook the pasta in a saucepan of boiling salted water until *al dente*. Remove and arrange the sheets on a tray to prevent them sticking. Blanch the spinach in the same pan of boiling water for 30 seconds. Remove with tongs, transfer to a colander and drain well.

3   To assemble, lay a pasta rectangle on each of four ovenproof serving plates. Spread half the mascarpone over the pasta sheets. Top with half the spinach and half the seafood sauce. Sprinkle with one third of the parmesan. Repeat to give two layers, finishing with a third pasta sheet. Sprinkle with the remaining cheese. Place under a grill (broiler) for 2 minutes, or until the cheese is slightly melted.

Ravioli with Prawns and Makrut Leaf Sauce

Serves 4

60 g (2¹/₄ oz) butter
4 garlic cloves, crushed
750 g (1¹/₂ lb) raw prawns (shrimp), peeled and deveined
1¹/₂ tablespoons plain (all-purpose) flour
375 ml (12 fl oz/1¹/₂ cups) fish stock
500 ml (17 fl oz/2 cups) pouring cream
5 makrut (kaffir lime) leaves, shredded
600 g (1 lb 5 oz) seafood ravioli
3 teaspoons fish sauce

1 Melt the butter in a deep large frying pan and cook the garlic over medium heat for 1 minute. Add the prawns and cook for 3–4 minutes, or until they turn pink and are cooked through. Remove from the pan, leaving any juices in the pan. Add the flour and stir for 1 minute, or until light golden. Gradually stir in the stock, then add the cream and makrut leaves. Reduce the heat and simmer for 10 minutes to slightly thicken.

2 Meanwhile, cook the pasta in a saucepan of boiling salted water until *al dente*. Drain and return to the pan to keep warm. Stir the fish sauce through the cream sauce. Add the prawns and stir until warmed through. Divide the pasta among four warm serving plates and spoon on the prawns and sauce. Season to taste with salt and cracked black pepper and serve immediately.

Baked Seafood Pasta

Serves 4–6

250 g (9 oz) lasagne sheets
125 g (4½ oz) butter
1 leek, sliced
90 g (3 oz/⅔ cup) plain (all-purpose) flour
500 ml (17 fl oz/2 cups) milk
500 ml (17 fl oz/2 cups) dry white wine
125 g (4 oz/1 cup) grated cheddar cheese
500 g (1 lb 2 oz) boneless fish fillets, chopped
125 g (4½ oz) scallops, cleaned, chopped
500 g (1 lb 2 oz) raw prawns (shrimp), peeled and deveined, chopped
125 ml (4 fl oz/½ cup) pouring cream
60 g (2 oz/½ cup) grated parmesan cheese
2 tablespoons chopped flat-leaf (Italian) parsley

1   Preheat the oven to 180°C (350°F/Gas 4). Line a greased shallow 24 x 30 cm (10 x 12 in) ovenproof dish with lasagne sheets, breaking them to fill any gaps.

2   Melt the butter in a large saucepan and cook the leek, stirring, for 1 minute. Add the flour and cook, stirring, for 1 minute. Remove from the heat and stir in the milk and wine until smooth. Return to the heat and stir until thick. Simmer for 3 minutes. Stir in the cheddar cheese and seafood, season and simmer for 1 minute.

3   Spoon half the seafood sauce over the lasagne sheets. Top with a layer of lasagne sheets. Continue layering, finishing with lasagne sheets.

4   Pour the cream over the top. Sprinkle with the combined parmesan and parsley and bake for 30 minutes, or until bubbling and golden.

Seafood Spaghetti Paper Parcels

Makes 6

185 g (6¹/2 oz) thin spaghetti
4 ripe roma (plum) tomatoes
1 tablespoon olive oil
4 spring onions (scallions), finely chopped
1 celery stick, finely chopped
80 ml (2³/4 fl oz/¹/3 cup) white wine
125 ml (4 fl oz/¹/2 cup) tomato pasta sauce
4 gherkins (pickles), finely diced
2 tablespoons drained capers, chopped
6 x 175 g (6 oz) pieces skinless salmon fillet or ocean trout, boned
6 large dill sprigs
shredded zest of 2 lemons
30 g (1 oz) butter, cut into small cubes

1 Preheat the oven to 180°C (350°F/Gas 4). Cook the pasta in a
   saucepan of boiling salted water until *al dente*. Drain and run under
   cold water. Transfer to a bowl.

2 Score a cross in the base of each tomato. Place in a heatproof bowl
   and cover with boiling water. Leave for 1 minute. Transfer to cold
   water, drain and peel the skin away from the cross. Halve each
   tomato, scoop out the seeds and chop the flesh.

3 Heat the oil in a frying pan. Add the spring onion and celery
   and stir for 2 minutes. Add the tomato and wine and bring to the
   boil. Boil for 3 minutes to reduce. Reduce the heat and stir in the
   pasta sauce, gherkins and capers. Season well. Mix well through
   the pasta.

4 To assemble, cut six 30 cm (12 in) square sheets (depending on the shape of your fish) of baking paper and brush the outside edges with oil. Divide the pasta among the sheets, using a fork to curl the pasta. Place a piece of salmon on top of each, then top with dill and lemon zest. Divide the butter among the parcels.

5 Fold into parcels, turning over twice at the top to seal. Tuck the ends under and bake on a baking tray for 20 minutes. To serve, cut or pull open the parcel and serve in the paper.

The parcels can be assembled a few hours ahead and refrigerated until required. If you do this, allow a couple of extra minutes cooking.

Conchiglie with Clams

Serves 4

2 tablespoons salt
2 tablespoons plain (all-purpose) flour
1 kg (2 lb 4 oz) clams or pipis
500 g (1 lb 2 oz) conchiglie
1 tablespoon olive oil
2 garlic cloves, crushed
850 g (1 lb 14 oz) tinned crushed tomatoes
60 ml (2 fl oz/$1/4$ cup) red wine
2 tablespoons chopped flat-leaf (Italian) parsley
1 teaspoon sugar

1 Blend the salt and plain flour with enough water to make a paste. Add to a large pan of cold water and soak the shellfish overnight. This will draw out sand from inside the shells. Scrub the shells well. Rinse and drain.

2 Cook the conchiglie in a saucepan of boiling salted water until *al dente*. Drain and return to the pan to keep warm.

3 Meanwhile, heat the oil in a large saucepan. Add the garlic and cook over low heat for 30 seconds. Add the tomatoes, wine, parsley and sugar and season. Stir and bring to the boil. Reduce the heat and simmer, stirring occasionally, for 5 minutes.

4 Add the clams to the sauce and cook for 3–5 minutes, stirring occasionally, until opened. Discard any clams that do not open. Serve over the pasta.

Spaghetti Vongole

Serves 4

2 tablespoons olive oil
3 garlic cloves, crushed
pinch of chilli flakes
1 teaspoon chopped flat-leaf (Italian) parsley
125 ml (4 fl oz) dry white wine
800 g (1 lb 12 oz) tinned chopped tomatoes
1 kg (2 lb 4 oz) clams
1 large handful finely chopped flat-leaf (Italian) parsley
400 g (14 oz) spaghetti or linguine
1/2 teaspoon grated lemon zest
lemon wedges, to serve

1 Heat the oil in a deep frying pan. Add the garlic and chilli and cook over low heat for 30 seconds. Add the parsley, wine and tomato. Increase the heat and boil, stirring, for 10 minutes, or until the liquid is reduced by half.

2 Scrub the clams and rinse well under running water. Discard any that are broken or cracked or do not close when tapped on the work surface. Add to the pan. Cover, increase the heat and cook for 3–5 minutes, or until the clams open. Shake the pan often. Remove the clams from the pan, discarding any that haven't opened. Stir in the parsley and season. Boil until thick. Set 12 clams aside and extract the meat from the rest.

3 Cook the pasta in a saucepan of boiling salted water until *al dente*. Drain and stir through the sauce. Add the lemon zest, reserved clams and clam meat and toss well. Serve with the lemon wedges.

Spaghetti alla Puttanesca

Serves 4

80 ml (2¹/₂ fl oz/¹/₃ cup olive oil
1 small onion, finely chopped
2 garlic cloves, finely sliced
1 small red chilli, cored, seeded and sliced
6 anchovy fillets, finely chopped
400 g (14 oz) tinned chopped tomatoes
1 tablespoon finely chopped oregano
100 g (3¹/₂ oz) pitted black olives, halved
1 tablespoon capers
400 g (14 oz) spaghetti

1 Heat the olive oil in a large saucepan. Add the onion, garlic and chilli and fry gently for about 6 minutes, or until the onion is soft. Add the anchovies and cook, stirring, until well mixed.

2 Add the tomato, oregano, olives and capers and bring to the boil. Reduce the heat, season and leave to simmer.

3 Meanwhile, cook the pasta in a saucepan of boiling salted water until *al dente*. Drain, toss well with the sauce and serve immediately.

Salmon and Ricotta-stuffed Conchiglione

Serves 4

200 g (7 oz) conchiglione
425 g (14 oz) tinned red salmon, drained, bones removed, flaked
500 g (1 lb 2 oz) ricotta cheese
1 tablespoon chopped flat-leaf (Italian) parsley
3 tablespoons chopped chives
1 1/2 celery stalks, finely chopped
90 g (3 oz/3/4 cup) grated cheddar cheese
185 ml (6 fl oz/3/4 cup) pouring cream
30 g (1 oz/1/4 cup) grated parmesan cheese

1 Preheat the oven to 180°C (350°F/Gas 4). Cook the pasta in a saucepan of boiling salted water until *al dente*. Drain and return to the pan to keep warm.

2 Combine the salmon, ricotta, parsley, chives, celery and cheddar in a bowl and season to taste with salt and cracked black pepper.

3 Place 2 teaspoons of filling in each shell and arrange in a single layer in a 3 litre (104 fl oz/12 cup) ovenproof dish. Pour on the cream and sprinkle with parmesan. Cover with foil and bake for 20 minutes, then remove the foil and return to the oven for 15 minutes, or until golden brown. Serve with the sauce spooned over the pasta.

Salmon with Lemon Cannelloni

Serves 4-6

FILLING

415 g (14³/₄ oz) tinned pink salmon

250 g (9 oz) ricotta cheese

1 tablespoon lemon juice

1 egg yolk, lightly beaten

2 tablespoons finely chopped onion

SAUCE

125 g (4¹/₂ oz) butter

85 g (3 oz/²/₃ cup) plain (all-purpose) flour

685 ml (23¹/₂ fl oz/2³/₄ cups) milk

1 teaspoon finely grated lemon zest

¹/₄ teaspoon ground nutmeg

16 cannelloni tubes

1–2 tablespoons chopped dill, to garnish

1 Drain the salmon, reserving the liquid for the sauce. Remove and discard the skin and bones. Flake the salmon flesh and mix with the ricotta, lemon juice, egg yolk and onion in a bowl. Add a little salt and pepper, to taste.

2 To make the sauce, melt the butter in a saucepan over low heat. Stir in the flour and cook for 1 minute, or until pale and foaming. Remove from the heat and gradually stir in the milk. Return to the heat and stir constantly until the sauce boils and thickens. Reduce the heat and simmer for 2 minutes. Add the reserved salmon liquid, lemon zest, nutmeg and salt and pepper, to taste. Set aside to cool.

3   Preheat the oven to 180°C (350°F/Gas 4). Fill the cannelloni tubes
    with the filling, using a small spoon or piping bag. Spread one third
    of the sauce over the base of a shallow ovenproof dish, then sit
    the cannelloni tubes in the dish side by side. Pour the remaining
    sauce over the top, covering all the exposed pasta. Bake for about
    30 minutes, until bubbly. Serve garnished with the dill.

Prawn Ravioli with Basil Butter

Serves 4

500 g (1 lb 2 oz) raw prawns (shrimp)
1 tablespoon chopped chives
1 egg white, lightly beaten
350 ml (12 fl oz) pouring cream
200 g (7 oz) packet gow gee wrappers
1 egg, lightly beaten

BASIL BUTTER
90 g (3 1/4 oz) butter
1 garlic clove, crushed
1 small handful basil leaves, finely shredded
40 g (1 1/2 oz) pine nuts

1   Peel the prawns and pull out the dark vein from each prawn back, starting at the head end. Put the prawns in a food processor with the chives and egg white and process until smooth. Season with salt and pepper. Add the cream, being careful not to overprocess or the mixture will curdle. Transfer to a bowl, cover and chill for 30 minutes.

2   Place 2–3 teaspoons of the prawn mixture in the centre of half the gow gee wrappers. Brush the edges with beaten egg, then cover with the remaining wrappers. Press the edges to seal. Add in batches to a large saucepan of boiling water and cook each batch for 4 minutes. Drain and divide among 4 serving plates.

3   To make the basil butter, melt the butter gently in a saucepan, add the garlic and stir until fragrant. Add the shredded basil, pine nuts and a little black pepper, and cook until the butter turns a nutty brown colour. Drizzle the butter over the pasta. Serve immediately.

Farfalle with Tuna, Mushrooms and Cream

Serves 4

60 g (2 oz) butter
1 tablespoon olive oil
1 onion, chopped
1 garlic clove, crushed
125 g (4 1/2 oz) button mushrooms, sliced
250 ml (9 fl oz/1 cup) pouring cream
450 g (1 lb) tinned tuna in brine, drained and flaked
1 tablespoon lemon juice
1 tablespoon chopped flat-leaf (Italian) parsley
500 g (1 lb 2 oz) farfalle

1   Heat the butter and olive oil in a large frying pan. Add the onion and garlic to the pan and stir over low heat for 3–5 minutes, until the onion is soft.

2   Add the mushrooms to the pan and cook for 2 minutes. Pour in the cream, bring to the boil then reduce the heat and simmer until the sauce begins to thicken. Add the tuna, lemon juice and parsley and stir until heated through. Add salt and pepper to taste.

3   Meanwhile, cook the farfalle in a saucepan of boiling salted water until *al dente*. Drain and return to the pan. Add the sauce to the pasta and toss to combine. Serve immediately.

Spaghetti and Mussels in Tomato and Fresh Herb Sauce

Serves 4

1.5 kg (3 lb 5 oz) black mussels
2 tablespoons olive oil
1 onion, finely sliced
2 garlic cloves, crushed
425 g (14 oz) tinned crushed tomatoes
250 ml (9 fl oz/1 cup) white wine
1 tablespoon chopped basil
2 tablespoons chopped flat-leaf (Italian) parsley
500 g (1 lb 2 oz) spaghetti

1 Remove the beards from the mussels and scrub away any grit. Discard any opened or damaged mussels. Rinse well, then refrigerate.

2 Heat the oil in a large saucepan, add the onion and garlic and stir over low heat for 5 minutes, or until the onion is tender. Add the tomato and wine and season, to taste. Bring to the boil, then reduce the heat and simmer for 15–20 minutes, or until the sauce begins to thicken.

3 Add the mussels to the pan, cover and simmer for 4–5 minutes, shaking the pan occasionally, or until the mussels are cooked. Discard any unopened mussels. Stir in the basil and parsley.

4 Meanwhile, cook the spaghetti in a saucepan of boiling salted water until *al dente*, then drain. Serve the mussels and sauce over the pasta.

Tagliatelle with Prawns and Cream

Serves 4

500 g (1 lb 2 oz) raw prawns (shrimp)
500 g (1 lb 2 oz) tagliatelle
60 g (2 oz) butter
6 spring onions (scallions), finely chopped
60 ml (2 fl oz/^{1}/4 cup) brandy
315 ml (10^3/4 fl oz/1^1/4 cups) thick (double/heavy) cream
1 tablespoon chopped thyme
15 g (^{1}/2 oz/^{1}/2 cup) finely chopped flat-leaf (Italian) parsley
grated parmesan cheese, to serve

1   Peel the prawns, leaving the tails intact. Gently pull out the dark vein
from each prawn.

2   Cook the tagliatelle in a saucepan of boiling salted water until
al dente. Drain and return to the pan to keep warm.

3   Meanwhile, melt the butter in a large heavy-based frying pan. Add
the spring onion and stir for 2 minutes. Add the prawns and stir for
2 minutes, or until the prawns just start to change colour. Remove
the prawns from the pan and set aside.

4   Add the brandy to the pan and boil for 2 minutes, or until the brandy
is reduced by half. Stir in the cream and add the thyme and half
the parsley. Season with freshly ground black pepper. Simmer for
5 minutes, or until the sauce begins to thicken. Return the prawns
to the sauce and cook for 2 minutes. Season well.

5   Toss the sauce through the pasta. Sprinkle with the remaining parsley
and grated parmesan.

Spinach and Ricotta Cannelloni Blue Chee

Pasta with vegetables

cchi Vegetarian Lasagne Pasta Primavera

Roast Pumpkin Sauce on Pappardelle

Serves 4

1.5 kg (3 lb) butternut pumpkin (squash), cut into small cubes
4 garlic cloves, crushed
3 teaspoons thyme leaves
100 ml (3½ fl oz) olive oil
500 g (1 lb 2 oz) pappardelle
2 tablespoons pouring cream
185 ml (6 fl oz/¾ cup) chicken stock
30 g (1 oz) shaved parmesan cheese

1 Preheat the oven to 200°C (400°F/Gas 6). Place the pumpkin, garlic, thyme and 60 ml (2 fl oz/¼ cup) of the olive oil in a bowl and toss together. Season with salt, transfer to a baking tray and cook for 30 minutes, or until tender and golden.

2 Meanwhile, cook the pasta in a saucepan of boiling salted water until *al dente*. Drain and return to the pan to keep warm. Toss through the remaining oil.

3 Place the pumpkin and cream in a food processor or blender and process until smooth. Add the hot stock and process until smooth. Season with salt and cracked black pepper and gently toss through the pasta. Serve with parmesan.

The sauce becomes thick on standing, so serve immediately.

Penne with Mushroom and Herb Sauce

Serves 4

2 tablespoons olive oil
500 g (1 lb 2 oz) button mushrooms, sliced
2 garlic cloves, crushed
2 teaspoons chopped marjoram
125 ml (4 fl oz/^{1}/$_2$ cup) dry white white
80 ml (2^3/$_4$ fl oz/^{1}/$_3$ cup) pouring cream
375 g (13 oz) penne
1 tablespoon lemon juice
1 teaspoon finely grated lemon zest
2 tablespoons chopped flat-leaf (Italian) parsley
60 g (2 oz/^{1}/$_2$ cup) grated parmesan cheese

1   Heat the oil in a large heavy-based frying pan over high heat. Add the mushrooms and cook for 3 minutes, stirring constantly. Add the garlic and marjoram and cook for 2 minutes.

2   Add the dry white wine, reduce the heat and simmer for 5 minutes, or until nearly all the liquid has evaporated. Stir in the cream and continue to cook over low heat for 5 minutes, or until the sauce has thickened.

3   Meanwhile, cook the pasta in a saucepan of boiling salted water until *al dente*. Drain and return to the pan to keep warm.

4   Add the lemon juice, zest, parsley and half the parmesan to the sauce. Season to taste. Toss the penne through the sauce and sprinkle with the remaining parmesan.

Fusilli with Baby Spinach, Roasted Pumpkin and Tomato

Serves 4

750 g (1 lb 10 oz) pumpkin (winter squash)
2 tablespoons olive oil
16 unpeeled garlic cloves
250 g (9 oz) cherry tomatoes, halved
500 g (1 lb 2 oz) fusilli
200 g (7 oz) baby English spinach leaves
200 g (7 oz) marinated Persian feta cheese
60 ml (2 fl oz/¼ cup) sherry vinegar
2 tablespoons walnut oil

1 Preheat the oven to 200°C (400°F/Gas 6). Cut the pumpkin into large cubes, place in a roasting tin and drizzle with oil. Roast for 30 minutes, then add the garlic. Arrange the tomatoes on a baking tray. Put all the vegetables in the oven and roast for 10–15 minutes, or until tender.

2 Cook the pasta in a saucepan of boiling salted water until *al dente*. Drain and return to the pan to keep warm.

3 Toss together the pasta, tomatoes, pumpkin, garlic and spinach.

4 Drain the feta, reserving 60 ml (2 fl oz/¼ cup) marinade. Whisk this with the vinegar and walnut oil. Pour over the pasta and sprinkle with feta.

Rotelle with Chickpeas, Tomato and Parsley

Serves 4

375 g (13 oz) rotelle
1 tablespoon ground cumin
125 ml (4 fl oz/$1/2$ cup) olive oil
1 red onion, halved and thinly sliced
3 garlic cloves, crushed
400 g (14 oz) tinned chickpeas, drained
3 large tomatoes, diced
15 g ($1/2$ oz/$1/2$ cup) chopped flat-leaf (Italian) parsley
60 ml (2 fl oz/$1/4$ cup) lemon juice

1 Cook the pasta in a saucepan of boiling salted water until *al dente*. Drain and return to the pan to keep warm.

2 Meanwhile, heat a large frying pan over medium heat. Add the cumin and cook, tossing, for 1 minute, or until fragrant. Remove from the pan. Heat half the oil in the same pan and cook the onion over medium heat for 2–3 minutes, or until soft. Stir in the garlic, chickpeas, tomato and parsley and stir until warmed through. Gently toss through the pasta.

3 Place the lemon juice, cumin and remaining oil in a jar with a lid and shake together well. Add the dressing to the saucepan with the pasta and chickpea mixture. Stir over low heat until warmed through. Season well with salt and cracked black pepper.

Vegetarian Lasagne

Serves 8

500 g (1 lb 2 oz) fresh spinach lasagne sheets
30 g (1 oz/^{1}/2 cup) basil leaves, coarsely chopped
2 tablespoons fresh breadcrumbs
3 tablespoons pine nuts
2 teaspoons smoked paprika
20 g (^{3}/4 oz) grated parmesan cheese

RICOTTA FILLING
750 g (1 lb 10 oz) ricotta cheese
50 g (1^3/4 oz/^{1}/2 cup) grated parmesan cheese
pinch of nutmeg

TOMATO SAUCE
1 tablespoon olive oil
2 onions, chopped
2 garlic cloves, crushed
800 g (1 lb 12 oz) tinned crushed tomatoes
1 tablespoon tomato paste (concentrated purée)

BECHAMEL SAUCE
60 g (2^1/4 oz) butter
60 g (2^1/4 oz/^{1}/2 cup) plain (all-purpose) flour
500 ml (17 fl oz/2 cups) milk
2 eggs, lightly beaten
30 g (1 oz/^{1}/3 cup) grated parmesan cheese

1 Lightly grease a 25 x 32 cm (10 x 13 in) baking dish. Cut the lasagne
sheets into large pieces. Cook the lasagne, 1–2 sheets at a time, in a
saucepan of boiling water for 3 minutes. Remove the sheets carefully

with two spatulas or wooden spoons and lay out flat on a damp tea towel (dish towel).

2 To make the ricotta filling, put the ricotta and parmesan cheeses and nutmeg in a bowl and mix together well. Season with black pepper and set aside.

3 To make the tomato sauce, heat the oil in a frying pan. Add the onion and cook for about 10 minutes, stirring occasionally, until very soft. Add the garlic and cook for a further 1 minute. Add the tomato and tomato paste and stir until well combined. Stir until the mixture comes to the boil. Reduce the heat and simmer uncovered for 15 minutes, or until thickened, stirring occasionally.

4 To make the béchamel sauce, heat the butter in a small saucepan. When starting to foam, add the flour and stir for 3 minutes, or until just coloured. Remove from the heat. Add the milk gradually, stirring after each addition, then return to the heat and stir until the sauce boils and thickens. Remove from the heat and stir in the eggs. Return to the heat and stir until almost boiling. Add the cheese and season to taste. Put plastic wrap onto the surface to prevent a skin forming. Preheat the oven to 200°C (400°F/Gas 6).

5 Put a layer of lasagne sheets in the dish. Spread with a third of the ricotta filling, sprinkle with basil, then top with a third of the tomato sauce. Repeat the layers, finishing with pasta.

6 Pour over the béchamel sauce, spread until smooth, then sprinkle with the combined breadcrumbs, pine nuts, paprika and parmesan. Bake for 45 minutes, or until browned. Leave to stand for 10 minutes before serving.

Penne with Rocket and Mushrooms

Serves 4

15 g (1/2 oz) dried porcini mushrooms
375 g (13 oz) penne
1 tablespoon butter
60 ml (2 fl oz/1/4 cup) extra virgin olive oil
2 garlic cloves, crushed
250 g (9 oz) button mushrooms, sliced
60 ml (2 fl oz/1/4 cup) lemon juice
30 g (1 oz/1/3 cup) grated parmesan cheese
90 g (31/4 oz) baby rocket (arugula) leaves

1 Soak the porcini mushrooms in 80 ml (23/4 fl oz/1/3 cup) boiling water for 10 minutes to soften. Cook the pasta in a saucepan of boiling salted water until *al dente*. Drain and return to the pan to keep warm.

2 Meanwhile, heat the butter and oil in a frying pan over medium heat. Add the garlic and button mushrooms and cook for 4 minutes, tossing occasionally. Drain the porcini mushrooms, reserving the soaking liquid. Chop the mushrooms, then add to the frying pan with the soaking liquid. Bring to a simmer.

3 Add the mushroom mixture, lemon juice and parmesan to the saucepan with the pasta and toss together. Season to taste with salt and cracked black pepper. Toss through the rocket just before serving.

Cotelli with Spring Vegetables

Serves 4

500 g (1 lb 2 oz) cotelli
300 g (10^1/$_2$ oz/2 cups) frozen peas
300 g (10^1/$_2$ oz/2 cups) frozen broad beans
80 ml (2^3/$_4$ fl oz/^{1}/$_3$ cup) olive oil
6 spring onions (scallions), cut into short pieces
2 garlic cloves, finely chopped
250 ml (9 fl oz/1 cup) chicken stock
12 asparagus spears, chopped
1 lemon

1 Cook the cotelli in a saucepan of boiling salted water until *al dente*. Drain and return to the pan to keep warm.

2 Meanwhile, cook the peas in a saucepan of boiling water for 1–2 minutes, or until tender. Remove with a slotted spoon and plunge into cold water. Add the broad beans to the same saucepan of boiling water. Cook for 1–2 minutes, then drain and plunge into cold water. Remove and slip out of their skins.

3 Heat 2 tablespoons of the oil in a frying pan. Add the spring onion and garlic and cook over medium heat for 2 minutes, or until softened. Pour in the stock and cook for 5 minutes, or until reduced. Add the asparagus and cook for 3–4 minutes, or until bright green and tender. Stir in the peas and broad beans and cook for 3 minutes to heat through.

4 Toss the remaining oil through the pasta, then add the vegetable mixture, ^{1}/$_2$ teaspoon grated lemon zest and 60 ml (2 fl oz/^{1}/$_4$ cup) lemon juice. Season and toss together.

Potato Gnocchi with Tomato Olive Sauce

Serves 4

500 g (1 lb 2 oz) fresh potato gnocchi
2 tablespoons oil
1 leek, sliced
250 ml (9 fl oz/1 cup) tomato pasta sauce
170 ml (5^1/2 fl oz/^{2}/3 cup) vegetable stock
60 g (2 oz/^{1}/3 cup) chopped black olives
6 anchovies, chopped

1 Cook the gnocchi in a saucepan of boiling salted water until they float to the surface. Lift out with a slotted spoon.

2 Meanwhile, heat the oil in a large saucepan and add the leek. Stir over medium heat for 2 minutes, or until tender. Add the tomato sauce, stock, olives and anchovies and stir for 5 minutes to heat through. Serve over the gnocchi.

The sauce will keep for a day, covered, in the refrigerator.

Pasta Pronto

Serves 4

2 tablespoons extra virgin olive oil
4 garlic cloves, finely chopped
1 small fresh red chilli, finely chopped
1.2 kg (2 lb 10 oz) tinned crushed tomatoes
1 teaspoon sugar
80 ml (2¾ fl oz/⅓ cup) dry white wine
3 tablespoons chopped basil
400 g (14 oz) vermicelli
30 g (1 oz) shaved parmesan cheese, to serve

1 Heat the oil in a large deep frying pan and cook the garlic and chilli for 1 minute. Add the tomato, sugar, wine, herbs and 440 ml (14 fl oz/1¾ cups) water. Bring to the boil and season.

2 Reduce the heat to medium and add the pasta, breaking the strands if they are too long. Cook, stirring often, for 10 minutes, or until *al dente*. Season and serve with shaved parmesan.

Spinach and Ricotta Cannelloni

Serves 4-6

375 g (13 oz) fresh lasagne sheets

2 tablespoons olive oil

1 large onion, finely chopped

1–2 garlic cloves, crushed

2 large bunches English spinach, finely chopped

650 g (1 lb 5 oz) ricotta cheese, beaten

2 eggs, beaten

1/4 teaspoon freshly ground nutmeg

150 g (5 1/2 oz) grated mozzarella cheese

TOMATO SAUCE

1 tablespoon olive oil

1 onion, chopped

2 garlic cloves, finely chopped

500 g (1 lb 2 oz) ripe tomatoes, chopped

2 tablespoons tomato paste (concentrated purée)

1 teaspoon soft brown sugar

1   Cut the lasagne sheets into 15 even-sized pieces and trim lengthways. Cook the lasagne, 1–2 sheets at a time, in a saucepan of boiling water until just softened. Remove the sheets carefully with two spatulas or wooden spoons and lay out flat on a damp tea towel (dish towel).

2   Heat the oil in a heavy-based frying pan. Cook the onion and garlic until golden, stirring regularly. Add the spinach and cook for 2 minutes. Cover with a tight-fitting lid and let the spinach steam for 5 minutes. Drain, removing as much liquid as possible. The

spinach must be quite dry or the pasta will be soggy. Combine the spinach with the ricotta, eggs, nutmeg and season with salt and pepper. Mix well and set aside.

3 To make the tomato sauce, heat the oil in a frying pan and cook the onion and garlic for 10 minutes over low heat, stirring occasionally. Add the chopped tomatoes and their juice, tomato paste, sugar and 125 ml (4 fl oz/½ cup) water and season with salt and pepper. Bring the sauce to the boil, reduce the heat and simmer for 10 minutes.

4 Preheat the oven to 180°C (350°F/Gas 4) and lightly grease a large ovenproof dish. Spread about one-third of the tomato sauce over the base of the dish. Working with one piece of the lasagne at a time, spoon 2½ tablespoons of the spinach mixture down the centre of each sheet, leaving a border at each end. Roll up and lay seam-side down in the dish. Trim the ends to fit evenly if necessary. Spoon the remaining tomato sauce over the cannelloni and scatter the cheese over the top. Bake for 30–35 minutes, or until golden. Set aside for 10 minutes before serving.

You can also use ready-made cannelloni tubes.

Free-form Wild Mushroom Lasagne

Serves 4

10 g (1/4 oz) dried porcini mushrooms
350 g (11 oz) wild mushrooms (such as shiitake, oyster and Swiss brown)
30 g (1 oz) butter
1 small onion, halved and thinly sliced
1 tablespoon chopped thyme
3 egg yolks
125 ml (4 fl oz/1/2 cup) thick (double/heavy) cream
100 g (31/2 oz/1 cup) grated parmesan cheese
8 fresh lasagne sheets (10 x 25 cm/4 x 10 in)

1   Soak the porcini in 60 ml (2 fl oz/1/4 cup) boiling water for
15 minutes. Strain through a sieve, reserving the liquid. Cut the
larger of all the mushrooms in half. Heat the butter in a frying
pan. Cook the onion over medium heat for 1–2 minutes, or until
just soft. Add the thyme and mushrooms and cook for 1–2 minutes,
or until softened. Pour in the reserved mushroom liquid and cook
for 1–2 minutes, or until the liquid has evaporated. Set aside.

2   Beat the egg yolks, cream and half the parmesan in a large bowl.

3   Cook the lasagne, 1–2 sheets at a time, in a saucepan of boiling
water until just softened. Remove the sheets carefully with two
spatulas or wooden spoons and drain. Toss the sheets gently through
the egg mixture while hot. Reheat the mushrooms quickly.

4   To serve, place a sheet of folded lasagne on a plate, top with some
mushrooms, then another sheet of folded lasagne. Drizzle with any
remaining egg mixture and sprinkle with the remaining parmesan.

Beetroot Ravioli with a Sage Burnt Butter

Serves 4

340 g (11¹/2 oz) jar baby beetroots (beets) in sweet vinegar
40 g (1¹/2 oz) grated parmesan cheese
250 g (9 oz) ricotta cheese
750 g (1 lb 10 oz) fresh lasagne sheets (4 sheets)
fine cornmeal, for sprinkling
200 g (7 oz) butter, chopped
5 g (¹/8 oz/¹/2 cup) sage, torn
2 garlic cloves, crushed

1 Drain the beetroot, then grate into a bowl. Add the parmesan and ricotta and mix. Lay a sheet of pasta on a flat surface and place tablespoons of the ricotta mixture on the pasta to give 12 mounds. Flatten the mounds of filling slightly. Brush the edges of the pasta sheet and around each pile of ricotta mix with water.

2 Place a second sheet of pasta over the top and gently press around each mound to seal and enclose the filling. Using a pasta wheel or sharp knife, cut the pasta into 12 ravioli. Lay them out separately on a lined tray that has been sprinkled with the cornmeal. Repeat with the remaining filling and lasagne sheets to make 24 ravioli. Gently remove any excess air bubbles after cutting so that they are sealed.

3 Cook the ravioli in a saucepan of boiling salted water until *al dente*. Drain, divide among four plates and keep warm. Melt the butter in a saucepan. Cook for 3–4 minutes, or until golden brown. Remove from the heat, stir in the sage and garlic and spoon over the ravioli.

Olive and Eggplant Toss

Serves 4

500 g (1 lb 2 oz) fettucine or tagliatelle
185 g (6¹/₂ oz/1 cup) green olives
1 large eggplant (aubergine)
2 tablespoons olive oil
2 garlic cloves, crushed
125 ml (4 fl oz/¹/₂ cup) lemon juice
2 tablespoons chopped flat-leaf (Italian) parsley
50 g (1³/₄ oz/¹/₂ cup) freshly grated parmesan cheese

1 Cook the pasta in a saucepan of boiling salted water until *al dente*. Drain and return to the pan to keep warm.

2 Meanwhile, chop the olives and cut the eggplant into small cubes.

3 Heat the oil in a heavy-based frying pan. Add the garlic and stir for 30 seconds. Add the eggplant and cook over medium heat, stirring frequently, for 6 minutes or until the eggplant is tender.

4 Add the olives, lemon juice and salt and pepper to the pan. Add the sauce to the pasta and toss well. Serve sprinkled with parsley and parmesan cheese.

Spaghettini with Herbs, Baby Spinach and Garlic Crumbs

Serves 4

375 g (13 oz) spaghettini
125 g (4¹/₂ oz) day-old crusty Italian bread, crusts removed
100 ml (3¹/₂ fl oz) extra virgin olive oil, plus extra for drizzling
4 garlic cloves, finely chopped
400 g (14 oz) baby spinach leaves
25 g (1 oz/¹/₂ cup) chopped flat-leaf (Italian) parsley
4 tablespoons chopped basil
1 tablespoon thyme leaves
30 g (1 oz) shaved parmesan cheese

1 Cook the pasta in a saucepan of boiling salted water until *al dente*. Drain, reserving 125 ml (4 fl oz/¹/₂ cup) of the pasta water. Return the pasta to the pan to keep warm.

2 Place the crustless bread in a food processor or blender and pulse until coarse breadcrumbs form. Heat 1 tablespoon of the oil in a saucepan. Add the breadcrumbs and half the garlic and toss for 2–3 minutes, or until lightly golden. Remove, then wipe clean the pan.

3 Heat 2 tablespoons of the oil in the same pan. Add the spinach and remaining garlic, toss together for 1 minute, then add the herbs. Cook, tossing, for a further 1 minute to wilt the herbs a little. Toss the spinach mixture through the pasta with the remaining oil and reserved pasta water. Divide among four serving bowls and scatter with the garlic crumbs. Serve hot sprinkled with parmesan and drizzled with extra virgin olive oil.

Tortellini Filled with Pumpkin and Sage

Serves 6

FILLING
900 g (2 lb) butternut pumpkin (squash), peeled and cubed
125 ml (4 fl oz/^{1}/2 cup) olive oil
1 small red onion, finely chopped
100 g (3^1/2 oz) ricotta cheese
1 egg yolk, beaten
25 g (1 oz) parmesan cheese, grated
1 teaspoon grated nutmeg
2 tablespoons chopped sage

750 g (1 lb 10 oz) fresh lasagne sheets (4 sheets)
1 egg
2 teaspoons milk

SAGE BUTTER
250 g (9 oz) butter
10 g sage leaves
grated parmesan cheese, to serve

1   To make the filling, preheat the oven to 190°C (375°F/Gas 5). Put the pumpkin in a roasting tin with half the olive oil and lots of salt and pepper. Bake in the oven for 40 minutes, or until soft.

2   Meanwhile, heat the remaining olive oil in a saucepan and gently cook the onion until soft. Put the onion and pumpkin in a bowl, draining off any excess oil, and mash well. Leave to cool, then crumble in the ricotta. Mix in the egg yolk, parmesan, nutmeg and sage. Season well.

3 To make the tortellini, cut the lasagne sheets into 8 cm (3¼ in) squares. Mix together the egg and milk to make an egg wash and brush lightly over the pasta just before you fill each one. Put a small teaspoon of filling in the middle of each square and fold it over diagonally to make a triangle, pressing down the corners. Pinch together the two corners on the longer side. (if you are not using the tortellini immediately, place them, well spaced out, on baking paper dusted with cornmeal and cover with a tea towel.

4 Cook the tortellini, in small batches, in a saucepan of boiling salted water until *al dente*. Remove and drain with a slotted spoon.

5 To make the sage butter, melt the butter slowly with the sage and leave to infuse for at least 5 minutes. Drizzle over the tortellini and serve with a sprinkling of parmesan.

If you are not using the tortellini immediately, place them, well spaced out, on baking paper dusted with cornmeal and cover with a tea towel (dish towel). They can be left for 1–2 hours before cooking — don't refrigerate or they will become damp.

Mushroom and Ricotta Cannelloni

Serves 4

500 g (1 lb 2 oz) button mushrooms
200 g (7 oz) fresh lasagne sheets
2 tablespoons olive oil
3 garlic cloves, crushed
2 tablespoons lemon juice
400 g (14 oz) ricotta cheese
3 tablespoons chopped basil
425 ml (15 fl oz) tomato pasta sauce
150 g (5$^{1}/_2$ oz/1 cup) grated mozzarella cheese

1 Preheat the oven to 180°C (350°F/Gas 4). Finely chop the
   mushrooms in a food processor. Cut the lasagne sheets into twelve
   13 x 16 cm (5 x 6$^{1}/_4$ in) rectangles.

2 Heat the oil in a large frying pan over medium heat. Add the garlic
   and mushrooms and cook, stirring, for 3 minutes. Add the lemon juice
   and cook for a further 2 minutes, or until softened. Transfer to a sieve
   over a bowl to collect the juices, pressing with a spoon to remove as
   much moisture as possible. Reserve.

3 Place the mushrooms in a bowl with the ricotta and basil. Season
   and mix well. Take a lasagne sheet and place heaped tablespoons of
   the mixture along one long edge. Roll up and arrange in a single layer
   in a greased 2 litre (70 fl oz/8 cup) shallow ovenproof dish. Repeat
   with the remaining mixture and lasagne sheets. Pour over the
   reserved mushroom cooking liquid, then pour over the pasta sauce.
   Sprinkle with cheese and bake for 25 minutes, or until golden.

Farfalle with Three Cheese Sauce

Serves 4

500 g (1 lb 2 oz) farfalle
30 g (1 oz) butter
90 g (3¼ oz) crumbled gorgonzola cheese
100 g (3½ oz) grated romano cheese
150 g (5½ oz) mascarpone
125 ml (4 fl oz/½ cup) pouring cream
2 tablespoons torn basil leaves
2 tablespoons roughly chopped, toasted walnuts

1 Cook the farfalle in a saucepan of boiling salted water until *al dente*. Drain and return to the pan to keep warm.

2 Meanwhile, melt the butter in a saucepan over medium heat. Add the gorgonzola cheese, romano cheese, mascarpone and cream. Stir to combine. Season with ground nutmeg and freshly ground black pepper. Simmer gently for 3–4 minutes.

3 Drain the pasta thoroughly and return to the pan. Add the cheese sauce to the pasta and toss to combine. Stir in the basil and walnuts. Serve immediately.

Cavatelli with Herb Sauce and Pecorino

serves 4

400 g (14 oz) cavatelli
90 g (3¼ oz) butter
2 garlic cloves, crushed
3 tablespoons chopped chives
3 tablespoons shredded basil
1 tablespoon shredded sage
1 teaspoon thyme
60 ml (2 fl oz/¼ cup) warm vegetable stock
60 g (2¼ oz) pecorino cheese, grated

1   Cook the cavatelli in a saucepan of boiling salted water until *al dente*. Drain and return to the pan to keep warm.

2   Meanwhile, heat the butter in a small saucepan over medium heat. Add the garlic and cook for 1 minute, or until fragrant. Add the chives, basil, sage and thyme and cook for a further minute.

3   Add the herb mixture and stock to the pasta. Return to the heat for 2–3 minutes, or until warmed through. Season to taste. Add the pecorino and mix well.

Pecorino is Italian sheep's milk cheese with a sharp flavour. If you can't find it, use parmesan instead.

Pumpkin and Pine Nut Tagliatelle

Serves 4

30 g (1 oz) butter
1 large onion, chopped
2 garlic cloves, crushed
375 ml (13 fl oz/1$\frac{1}{2}$ cups) vegetable stock
750 g (1 lb 10 oz) butternut pumpkin (squash), peeled and chopped
$\frac{1}{4}$ teaspoon ground nutmeg
250 ml (9 fl oz/1 cup) pouring cream
500 g (1 lb 2 oz) fresh tagliatelle
80 g (2$\frac{3}{4}$ oz/$\frac{1}{2}$ cup) pine nuts, toasted
2 tablespoons chopped chives
freshly grated parmesan cheese, to serve

1   Melt the butter in a large saucepan. Add the onion and cook for
3 minutes, or until soft. Add the garlic and cook for a further minute.
Stir in the vegetable stock and add the pumpkin. Bring to the boil,
reduce the heat slightly and cook until the pumpkin is tender.

2   Reduce the heat to very low and season with the nutmeg and
pepper. Stir in the cream until just warmed through. Transfer to a
food processor and process for about 30 seconds, until the mixture
forms a smooth sauce.

3   Meanwhile, cook the tagliatelle in a saucepan of boiling salted water
until *al dente*. Drain and return to the pan to keep warm.

4   Return the sauce to the pan and reheat. Add to the pasta with the
pine nuts and toss well. Serve sprinkled with chives and parmesan.

Blue Cheese Gnocchi

Serves 4

500 g (1 lb 2 oz) potatoes, quartered
150 g (5^{1}/$_{2}$ oz/1^{1}/$_{4}$ cups) plain (all-purpose) flour

SAUCE
300 ml (10^{1}/$_{2}$ fl oz) pouring cream
125 g (4^{1}/$_{2}$ oz) gorgonzola cheese, roughly chopped
2 tablespoons chopped chives

1 Cook the potatoes in boiling salted water for 15–20 minutes, or until tender. Stir through a generous amount of salt. Drain the potatoes, then mash until completely smooth. Transfer to a bowl.

2 Sprinkle the flour into the bowl with one hand while kneading it into the potato mixture with the other hand. Continue kneading until all the flour is worked in and the dough is smooth.

3 Divide the dough into three portions and roll each portion into a 2 cm (³/4 in) thick sausage. Cut into 2.5 cm (1 in) lengths and, using floured hands, press each gnocchi against a fork to flatten it and indent one side (the indentation helps the sauce to stick to the cooked gnocchi).

4 Bring a large saucepan of water to the boil. When rapidly boiling, drop in the gnocchi, then reduce the heat and simmer until the gnocchi rise to the surface. This will take 2–3 minutes. Lift the gnocchi out of the water with a slotted spoon and drain well. Keep warm on a serving dish.

5 Put the cream in a small saucepan and bring to the boil. Boil, stirring constantly, for about 5 minutes, or until the sauce has reduced by a third. Remove from the heat and stir through the cheese. Season and pour over the gnocchi. Scatter the chives over the top and serve immediately.

Spinach Ravioli with Semi-dried Tomatoes and Pine Nut Salsa

Serves 4

625 g (1 lb 6 oz) spinach ravioli

70 ml (2¼ fl oz) olive oil

60 g (2¼ oz/⅓ cup) pine nuts

150 g (5½ oz) semi-dried tomatoes, thinly sliced

270 g (9½ oz) jar roasted capsicums (peppers), drained and thinly sliced

2 tablespoons finely chopped flat-leaf (Italian) parsley

2 tablespoons finely chopped mint

1½ tablespoons balsamic vinegar

30 g (1 oz) shaved parmesan cheese

1   Cook the ravioli in a saucepan of boiling salted water until *al dente*. Drain and return to the pan to keep warm.

2   Heat ½ teaspoon of the oil in a frying pan and gently cook the pine nuts until golden. Remove from the pan and roughly chop.

3   Add the remaining oil to the pan and add the tomato, capsicum, parsley, mint and vinegar. Stir to warm through. Remove from the heat and season to taste. Stir in the pine nuts. Divide the pasta among four serving plates, spoon on the sauce and top with the parmesan. Serve immediately.

Gnocchi alla Romana

Serves 4

750 ml (26 fl oz/3 cups) milk
1/2 teaspoon ground nutmeg
90 g (3¼ oz/²/₃ cup) semolina
1 egg, beaten
150 g (5½ oz/1½ cups) grated parmesan cheese
60 g (2¼ oz) butter, melted
125 ml (4 fl oz/½ cup) pouring cream
75 g (2½ oz/½ cup) grated mozzarella cheese

1 Line a deep 30 x 20 cm (12 x 8 in) swiss roll tin (jelly roll tin) with baking paper.

2 Put the milk and half the nutmeg in a saucepan and season. Bring to the boil. Reduce the heat and gradually stir in the semolina. Cook, stirring occasionally, for 5–10 minutes or until very stiff. Remove from the heat. Add the egg and 90 g (3¼ oz/1 cup) parmesan and stir well. Spread in the tin and refrigerate for 1 hour, or until firm.

3 Preheat the oven to 180°C (350°F/Gas 4). Cut the semolina into rounds using a small floured biscuit (cookie) cutter. Arrange in a greased shallow casserole dish.

4 Pour the melted butter over the gnocchi, followed by the cream. Sprinkle with the remaining parmesan, mozzarella and nutmeg. Bake for 20–25 minutes or until golden.

Pumpkin, Basil and Ricotta Lasagne

Serves 4

650 g (1 lb 5 oz) pumpkin (winter squash)
2 tablespoons olive oil
500 g (1 lb 2 oz) ricotta cheese
60 g (2^1/$_4$ oz/^{1}/$_3$ cup) pine nuts, toasted
35 g (1 oz/^{3}/$_4$ cup) basil
2 garlic cloves, crushed
30 g (1 oz/^{1}/$_3$ cup) grated parmesan cheese
125 g (4^1/$_2$ oz) fresh lasagne sheets
185 g (6^1/$_2$ oz/1^1/$_4$ cups) grated mozzarella cheese

1 Preheat the oven to 180°C (350°F/Gas 4). Lightly grease a baking
   tray. Cut the pumpkin into thin slices and arrange in a single layer on
   the tray. Brush with oil and cook for 1 hour, or until softened, turning
   halfway through cooking.

2 Mix together the ricotta, pine nuts, basil, garlic and parmesan.

3 Brush a square 20 cm (8 in) ovenproof dish with oil. Cook the
   lasagne, 1–2 sheets at a time, in a saucepan of boiling water until
   just softened. Remove the sheets carefully with two spatulas or
   wooden spoons and lay out flat on a damp tea towel (dish towel).
   Arrange one-third of the pasta sheets over the base of the dish.
   Spread with the ricotta mixture. Top with half the remaining
   lasagne sheets.

4 Arrange the pumpkin over the pasta. Season and top with
   another layer of pasta sheets. Sprinkle with mozzarella. Bake for
   20–25 minutes, or until the cheese is golden. Allow to stand for
   10 minutes, then cut into squares to serve.

Cheese Tortellini with Capsicum and Almond Sauce

Serves 4

1 red capsicum (pepper)
1 yellow capsicum (pepper)
60 g (2 oz/^{2}/$_3$ cup) flaked almonds
8 spring onions (scallions), roughly chopped
2 garlic cloves, crushed
500 g (1 lb 2 oz) cheese tortellini
170 ml (5^1/$_2$ fl oz/^{2}/$_3$ cup) olive oil
30 g (1 oz/^{1}/$_3$ cup) finely grated pecorino cheese

1 Cut the capsicums into large pieces, removing the seeds and membrane. Place skin side up under a hot grill (broiler) until the skin blackens and blisters. Cool in a plastic bag, then peel away the skin. Spread the almonds on a baking tray and grill (broil) for 1–2 minutes, or until lightly toasted.

2 Put the capsicum, almonds, garlic and spring onion in a food processor and pulse until chopped.

3 Cook the tortellini in a saucepan of boiling salted water until *al dente*. Drain and return to the pan to keep warm. Toss the capsicum mixture through the pasta, then add the oil and cheese.

Tortellini with Mushroom Sauce

Serves 4

PASTA
250 g (9 oz/2 cups) plain (all-purpose) flour
3 eggs
1 tablespoon olive oil

FILLING
125 g (4½ oz) frozen spinach, thawed, excess liquid squeezed out
125 g (4½ oz) ricotta cheese
40 g (1½ oz) grated parmesan cheese
1 egg, beaten

SAUCE
1 tablespoon olive oil
1 garlic clove, crushed
125 g (4½ oz) mushrooms, sliced
250 ml (9 fl oz/1 cup) pouring cream
60 g (2¼ oz) grated parmesan cheese

60 g (2¼ oz) grated parmesan cheese, to serve
3 tablespoons finely chopped flat-leaf (Italian) parsley, to serve

1   To make the pasta, sift the flour and salt onto a board. Make a well in
    the centre of the flour. Whisk together the eggs, oil and 1 tablespoon
    water. Add this gradually to the flour, working in with your hands
    until the mixture forms a ball. Add a little more water if necessary.
    Knead on a lightly floured surface for 5 minutes, or until the dough is
    smooth and elastic. Put in a lightly oiled bowl. Cover with plastic
    wrap and leave for 30 minutes.

2 To make the filling, mix together the spinach, ricotta, parmesan, egg, and salt and pepper. Set aside.

3 To make the sauce, heat the oil in a frying pan. Add the garlic and stir over low heat for 30 seconds. Add the mushrooms and cook for 3 minutes. Pour in the cream. Remove from the heat.

4 Roll out the dough on a lightly floured surface until about 1 mm ($^1/_{16}$ in) thick. Using a floured cutter, cut into 5 cm (2 in) rounds. Spoon $^1/_2$ teaspoon of filling in the centre of each round. Brush a little water around the edge. Fold each round in half to form a semi-circle. Press the edges together firmly. Wrap each semi-circle around your forefinger to make a ring. Press the ends of the dough together firmly.

5 Cook the tortellini in batches in a saucepan of boiling salted water until *al dente*. Drain and return to the pan to keep warm.

6 Return the sauce to the heat. Bring to the boil, then reduce the heat and simmer for 3 minutes. Add the parmesan and salt and pepper and stir well. Toss the sauce and tortellini together. Mix together the parmesan and chopped parsley and serve as an accompaniment to the pasta.

Ricotta, Eggplant and Pasta Timbales

Makes 4

125 ml (4 fl oz/1/2 cup) light olive oil
1 large eggplant (aubergine), cut lengthways into thin slices
200 g (7 oz) macaroni
1 small onion, finely chopped
2 garlic cloves, crushed
400 g (14 oz) tinned diced tomatoes
400 g (14 oz) ricotta cheese
90 g (3 1/4 oz/1 cup) roughly grated parmesan cheese
15 g (1/2 oz/1/2 cup) shredded basil

1 Preheat the oven to 180°C (350°F/Gas 4). Heat 2 tablespoons of the oil in a frying pan. Cook the eggplant in batches over medium heat for 2 minutes each side, or until golden, adding 2 tablespoons of the oil with each batch. Remove and drain on paper towels.

2 Cook the macaroni in a saucepan of boiling salted water until *al dente*. Drain and return to the pan to keep warm.

3 Add the onion and garlic to the frying pan and cook over medium heat for 2–3 minutes, or until just golden. Add the tomato and cook for 5 minutes, or until the sauce is pulpy and most of the liquid has evaporated. Season.

4 Combine the ricotta, parmesan and basil in a large bowl, then mix in the pasta. Line four 375 ml (12 fl oz/1 1/2 cup) ramekins with eggplant, trimming to fit the base and sides. Top with half the pasta mix, pressing down firmly. Spoon on the tomato sauce, then cover with the remaining pasta mix. Bake for 10–15 minutes, or until heated through.

Zucchini Pasta Bake

Serves 4

200 g (7 oz) risoni
40 g (1 1/2 oz) butter
4 spring onions (scallions), thinly sliced
400 g (14 oz) zucchini (courgette), grated
4 eggs
125 ml (4 fl oz/ 1/2 cup) pouring cream
100 g (3 1/2 oz) ricotta cheese
100 g (3 1/2 oz/ 2/3 cup) grated mozzarella cheese
75 g (2 1/2 oz/ 3/4 cup) grated parmesan cheese

1 Preheat the oven to 180°C (350°F/Gas 4). Cook the risoni in a saucepan of boiling salted water until *al dente*. Drain and return to the pan to keep warm.

2 Meanwhile, heat the butter in a frying pan. Add the spring onion and cook for 1 minute, then add the zucchini and cook for 4 minutes, or until soft. Cool slightly.

3 Place the eggs, cream, ricotta, mozzarella, risoni and half of the parmesan in a bowl and mix well. Stir in the zucchini mixture, then season. Spoon the mixture into four 500 ml (17 fl oz/2 cup) greased ovenproof dishes, but do not fill to the brim. Sprinkle with the remaining parmesan and cook for 25–30 minutes, or until firm and golden.

Baked Macaroni with Butter Sauce

Serves 4

200 g (7 oz) macaroni
150 g (5¹/₂ oz) butter
30 g (1 oz/¹/₄ cup) plain (all-purpose) flour
600 ml (21 fl oz) milk
1 egg, lightly beaten
185 g (6¹/₂ oz/1¹/₂ cups) grated cheddar cheese
2 garlic cloves, crushed
2 ripe tomatoes, seeded and diced

1 Preheat the oven to 180°C (350°F/Gas 4). Lightly grease four shallow 250 ml (9 fl oz/1 cup) ovenproof dishes.

2 Cook the macaroni in a saucepan of boiling salted water until *al dente*. Drain and return to the pan to keep warm.

3 Melt 60 g (2¹/₄ oz) of the butter in a saucepan. Add the flour and cook, stirring, over low heat for 1 minute. Remove from the heat and add the milk. Return to the heat and cook, stirring, for 4 minutes, or until thick. Reduce the heat and simmer for 1 minute. Season.

4 Add the pasta, egg and two-thirds of the cheese. Stir well. Spoon into the dishes and sprinkle with the remaining cheese. Put the dishes in a roasting tin. Pour enough boiling water into the tin to come halfway up the sides of the dishes. Bake for 25 minutes, or until set. Remove from the roasting tin and allow to rest for 5 minutes.

5 To make the sauce, melt the remaining butter in a frying pan. Add the garlic and tomato and stir over medium heat for 2 minutes. Unmould the macaroni onto plates and spoon the warm sauce around the outside.

Penne with Pesto

Serves 4-6

500 g (1 lb 2 oz) penne
3 tablespoons pine nuts
100 g (3¹/₂ oz/2 cups) basil leaves
2 garlic cloves, peeled
¹/₂ teaspoon salt
60 g (2¹/₄ oz) grated parmesan cheese
40 g (1¹/₂ oz) grated pecorino cheese, optional
125 ml (4 fl oz/¹/₂ cup) olive oil

1 Cook the penne in a saucepan of boiling salted water until *al dente*. Drain and return to the pan to keep warm.

2 Meanwhile, toast the pine nuts in a dry heavy-based frying pan over low heat for 2–3 minutes, or until golden. Allow to cool. Process the pine nuts, basil leaves, garlic, salt and cheeses in a food processor for 20 seconds, or until finely chopped.

3 With the motor running, gradually add the oil in a thin steady stream until a paste is formed. Add freshly ground black pepper, to taste. Toss the sauce with the warm pasta.

Pesto sauce can be made up to one week in advance and refrigerated in an airtight container. Ensure the pesto is tightly packed and seal the surface with plastic wrap or pour a little extra oil over the top to prevent the pesto from turning black.

Individual Spinach and Leek Lasagnes

Serves 4

8 fresh lasagne sheets
8 roma (plum) tomatoes, halved
4 large field mushrooms, stalks removed
80 ml ($2^3/4$ fl oz/$^1/3$ cup) olive oil
1 tablespoon chopped thyme
60 g ($2^1/4$ oz) butter
2 large leeks, finely sliced
2 garlic cloves, crushed
500 g (1 lb 2 oz) packet frozen chopped English spinach, thawed
250 g (9 oz/1 cup) light sour cream
250 g (9 oz/1 cup) light cream
600 g (1 lb 5 oz) ricotta cheese
1 egg, lightly beaten
125 g ($4^1/2$ oz/1 cup) grated cheddar cheese

1 Preheat the oven to 200°C (400°F/Gas 6). Lightly grease four 500 ml (17 fl oz/2 cup) ovenproof dishes. Cut half the lasagne sheets to fit the bases of the dishes.

2 Place the tomatoes and mushrooms in a baking dish. Mix together the oil and thyme and drizzle over the tomato and mushroom. Season. Bake for 15 minutes, then turn over and bake for another 10 minutes, or until softened. Roughly chop.

3 Heat the butter in a frying pan, add the leek and garlic and cook over medium heat for 2–3 minutes, or until soft. Squeeze the liquid from the spinach and add to the leek mixture with the sour cream

and cream. Stir well, bring to the boil and cook for 5 minutes, or until reduced slightly. Stir in the tomato and mushroom.

4 Spoon half the spinach and leek mixture into the dishes. Cover with the remaining lasagne sheets, breaking them up as needed, and repeat with the remaining mixture. Spread with the combined ricotta and egg and sprinkle with cheddar. Bake for 20 minutes, or until golden.

Orzo and Greek Cheese Bake

Serves 6

415 g (14³/4 oz/2 cups) orzo
60 g (2¹/4 oz) butter
6 spring onions (scallions), chopped
450 g (1 lb) English spinach, trimmed and chopped
2 tablespoons plain (all-purpose) flour
1.25 litres (44 fl oz/5 cups) milk
250 g (9 oz) kefalotyri cheese, grated
250 g (9 oz) marinated feta cheese, drained
3 tablespoons chopped dill

1 Preheat the oven to 190°C (375°F/Gas 5). Cook the orzo in a saucepan of boiling salted water until *al dente*. Drain and return to the pan to keep warm.

2 Heat 1 tablespoon of the butter in a large saucepan over high heat. Cook the spring onion for 30 seconds. Add the spinach and stir for 1 minute, or until wilted. Season and stir into the pasta.

3 Melt the remaining butter in a saucepan over low heat. Stir in the flour and cook for 1 minute, or until pale and foaming. Remove from the heat and gradually stir in the milk. Return to the heat and stir constantly for 5 minutes, or until the sauce boils and thickens. Add two-thirds of the kefalotyri and all of the feta and stir for 2 minutes until melted. Remove from the heat and stir in the dill.

4 Combine the pasta mixture with the cheese sauce. Season to taste and pour into a lightly greased 2.5 litre (87 fl oz/10 cup) ovenproof dish. Sprinkle the remaining cheese on top and bake for 15 minutes, or until golden.

Fusilli, Tomato and Artichoke Grill

Serves 4

350 g (12 oz) fusilli
285 g (10 oz) jar marinated artichoke hearts, drained and chopped
2 tablespoons olive oil
250 ml (9 fl oz/1 cup) thick (double/heavy) cream
2 tablespoons chopped thyme
2 garlic cloves, crushed
75 g (2¹/2 oz/³/4 cup) grated parmesan cheese
200 g (7 oz) grated cheddar cheese
1 kg (2 lb 4 oz) tomatoes, thinly sliced

1   Cook the pasta in a saucepan of boiling salted water until *al dente*.
    Drain and return to the pan to keep warm. Grease a 23 x 30 cm
    (9 x 12 in) ovenproof dish.

2   Stir the artichoke, olive oil, cream, thyme, garlic, half the parmesan
    and 150 g (5¹/2 oz/1¹/4 cups) of the cheddar through the pasta and
    season well. Spread evenly into the prepared dish.

3   Arrange the tomatoes over the top, overlapping. Season and sprinkle
    with the remaining cheddar and parmesan. Grill (broil) for 6 minutes,
    or until browned.

Tagliatelle Pomodoro

Serves 4

500 g (1 lb 2 oz) tagliatelle
1¹/₂ tablespoons olive oil
1 onion, very finely chopped
800 g (1 lb 12 oz) tinned crushed tomatoes
1 small handful basil leaves

1 Cook the pasta in a saucepan of boiling salted water until *al dente*. Drain and return to the pan to keep warm.

2 Heat the oil in a large frying pan. Add the onion and cook over medium heat until softened. Stir in the tomato and simmer for 5–6 minutes, or until the sauce has reduced slightly and thickened. Season to taste. Stir in the basil leaves and cook for a further minute. Gently toss through the pasta and serve immediately.

Traditionally, pomodoro is served with tagliatelle. It can also be served with fettucine or angel hair pasta.

Spaghetti and Spinach Timbales

Serves 6

30 g (1 oz) butter
1 tablespoon olive oil
1 onion, chopped
500 g (1 lb 2 oz) English spinach, cooked
8 eggs, beaten
250 ml (9 fl oz/1 cup) pouring cream
100 g (3 1/2 oz) spaghetti, cooked
60 g (2 1/4 oz/1/2 cup) grated cheddar cheese
60 g (2 1/4 oz/1/2 cup) grated parmesan cheese

1 Preheat the oven to 180°C (350°F/Gas 4). Lightly grease six 250 ml (9 fl oz/1 cup) ramekins. Line the bases with baking (parchment) paper. Heat the butter and oil together in a frying pan. Add the onion and stir over low heat until tender. Add the spinach and cook for 1 minute. Remove from the heat and allow to cool. Whisk in the eggs and cream. Stir in the spaghetti, cheeses and salt and pepper. Spoon into the ramekins.

2 Place the ramekins in a roasting tin. Pour enough boiling water into the tin to come halfway up the sides of the ramekins. Bake for 30–35 minutes, or until set.

3 Allow the timbales to rest for 15 minutes, then run the point of a knife around the edge of each mould and unmould onto plates.

Potato Gnocchi and Tomato Sauce

Serves 4

500 g (l lb 2 oz) floury potatoes, unpeeled
1 egg yolk
60 g (2 1/4 oz) grated parmesan cheese
125 g (4 1/2 oz/1 cup) plain (all-purpose) flour

TOMATO SAUCE
425g (15 oz) tinned tomatoes
1 small onion, chopped
1 celery stick, chopped
1 small carrot, chopped
1 tablespoon shredded basil
1 teaspoon chopped thyme
1 garlic clove, crushed
1 teaspoon caster (superfine) sugar

1   Steam or boil the potatoes until just tender. Drain thoroughly and allow to cool for 10 minutes before peeling and mashing them.

2   Put the mashed potato into a large bowl. Mix in the egg yolk, parmesan, 1/4 teaspoon of salt and some black pepper. Slowly add flour until you have a slightly sticky dough. Knead for 5 minutes, adding more flour if necessary, until a smooth dough is formed.

3   Divide the dough into four portions and roll each portion on a lightly floured surface to form a sausage shape, about 2 cm (3/4 in) thick.

4   Cut the rolls into 2.5 cm (1 in) slices and shape each piece into an oval. Press each oval into the palm of your hand against a floured fork, to flatten slightly and indent one side with a pattern. As you

make the gnocchi, place them in a single layer on a baking tray and cover until ready to use.

5 To make the tomato sauce, combine all the ingredients with salt and pepper in a saucepan. Bring to the boil, reduce the heat to medium-low and simmer for 30 minutes, stirring occasionally. Allow to cool, then process in a food processor or blender, until smooth.

6 Cook the gnocchi in batches in a large saucepan of boiling salted water for 2 minutes, or until the gnocchi float to the surface. Drain well. Serve the gnocchi tossed through the sauce.

The gnocchi can be prepared several hours in advance and arranged on a tray in a single layer to prevent them sticking together. Cover and keep refrigerated. Gnocchi is traditionally made using potatoes baked in their skins. This results in a drier dough that is easy to work with, so if you have time you can use this method.

Tagliatelle with Feta, Tomato and Rocket

Serves 4

4 vine-ripened tomatoes
1 small red onion, finely chopped
4 tablespoons shredded basil
2 tablespoons olive oil
375 g (13 oz) tagliatelle
2 garlic cloves, finely chopped
150 g (5 1/2 oz) baby rocket (arugula) leaves
150 g (5 1/2 oz) soft feta cheese, crumbled

1 Score a cross in the base of each tomato, then place in a bowl of boiling water for 1 minute. Plunge into cold water and peel the skin away from the cross. Cut in half and remove the seeds with a teaspoon. Chop the flesh, then transfer to a bowl. Add the onion and basil, stir in 1 tablespoon of the oil and set aside.

2 Cook the pasta in a saucepan of boiling salted water until *al dente*. Drain, reserving 125 ml (4 fl oz/1/2 cup) of the pasta water. Return the pasta to the pan, add the remaining oil, the garlic and the reserved pasta water. Toss together over medium heat for 2 minutes to warm through. Stir in the tomato mixture, rocket and feta. Season to taste with salt and pepper. Divide among four serving plates and serve immediately.

Spaghetti Primavera

Serves 4

500 g (1 lb 2 oz) spaghetti
150 g (5¹/2 oz/1 cup) frozen broad beans
200 g (7 oz) sugar snap peas
150 g (5¹/2 oz) aparagus spears
30 g (1 oz) butter
250 ml (9 fl oz/1 cup) pouring cream
60 g (2¹/4 oz) grated parmesan cheese

1 Cook the pasta in a saucepan of boiling salted water until *al dente*. Drain and return to the pan to keep warm.

2 Cook the beans in boiling water for 2 minutes, then refresh in iced water and drain. Remove the skins from the broad beans.

3 Trim the stalks from the peas and snap the tough woody ends from the asparagus spears. Cut the asparagus into short lengths.

4 Melt the butter in a frying pan. Add the vegetables, cream and parmesan. Simmer gently for 3–4 minutes, or until the peas and asparagus are just tender. Season to taste. Pour the sauce over the warm pasta and toss. Serve immediately.

Fusilli with Roasted Tomatoes, Tapenade and Bocconcini

Serves 4-6

800 g (1 lb 12 oz) cherry or teardrop tomatoes (or a mixture of both), halved if they are large
500 g (1 lb 2 oz) fusilli
300 g (10½ oz) baby bocconcini cheese, sliced
1 tablespoon chopped thyme

TAPENADE
1½ tablespoons capers
2 small garlic cloves
185 g (6½ oz/1½ cups) sliced black olives
60 ml (2 fl oz/¼ cup) lemon juice
80 ml (2¾ fl oz/⅓ cup) extra virgin olive oil

1 Preheat the oven to 200°C (400°F/Gas 6). Place the tomatoes on a baking tray, sprinkle with salt and pepper and bake for 10 minutes, or until slightly dried.

2 To make the tapenade, place the capers, garlic, olives and lemon juice in a food processor and mix together. With the motor running, gradually add the oil until the mixture forms a smooth paste.

3 Cook the fusilli in a saucepan of boiling salted water until *al dente*. Drain and return to the pan to keep warm.

4 Toss the tapenade and bocconcini through the pasta. Top with the roasted tomatoes and thyme and serve immediately.

Ravioli with Roasted Red Capsicum Sauce

Serves 4

6 red capsicums (peppers)
625 g (1 lb 6 oz) ravioli
2 tablespoons olive oil
3 garlic cloves, crushed
2 leeks, thinly sliced
1 tablespoon chopped oregano
2 teaspoons soft brown sugar
250 ml (9 fl oz/1 cup) hot vegetable or chicken stock

1 Cut the capsicums into large pieces, removing the seeds and membrane. Cook, skin side up, under a hot grill (broiler) until the skin blackens and blisters. Cool in a plastic bag, then peel away the skin.

2 Cook the ravioli in a saucepan of boiling salted water until *al dente*. Drain and return to the pan to keep warm.

3 Meanwhile, heat the olive oil in a frying pan and cook the garlic and leek over medium heat for 3–4 minutes, or until softened. Add the oregano and brown sugar and stir for 1 minute.

4 Place the capsicum and leek mixture in a food processor or blender, season with salt and pepper and process until combined. Add the stock and process until smooth. Gently toss the sauce through the ravioli over low heat until warmed through. Divide among four bowls and serve immediately.

Fresh Vegetable Lasagne with Rocket

Serves 4

BALSAMIC SYRUP
80 ml (2³/4 fl oz/¹/3 cup) balsamic vinegar
1¹/2 tablespoons brown sugar

150 g (5¹/2 oz/1 cup) fresh or frozen peas
16 asparagus spears, trimmed and cut into short lengths
2 large zucchini (courgettes), cut into thin ribbons
2 fresh lasagne sheets
100 g (3¹/2 oz) rocket (arugula) leaves
2 handfuls basil, torn
2 tablespoons extra virgin olive oil
250 g (9 oz) low-fat ricotta cheese
150 g (5¹/2 oz) semi-dried tomatoes
parmesan cheese shavings, to serve

1 To make the syrup, place the vinegar and brown sugar in a small saucepan and stir over medium heat until the sugar dissolves. Reduce the heat and simmer for 3–4 minutes, or until the sauce becomes syrupy. Remove from the heat.

2 Bring a large saucepan of salted water to the boil. Blanch the peas, asparagus and zucchini in separate batches until just tender, removing each batch with a slotted spoon and refreshing in cold water. Reserve the cooking liquid and return to the boil.

3 Cook the lasagne sheets in the boiling water for 1–2 minutes, or until *al dente*. Refresh in cold water and drain well. Cut each sheet in half lengthways.

4 Toss the vegetables and the rocket with the basil and olive oil, then season.

5 To assemble, place one pasta strip on a serving plate — one–third on the centre of the plate and two–thirds overhanging one side. Place a small amount of the salad on the centre one–third, topped with some ricotta and tomato. Season lightly and fold over one–third of the lasagne sheet. Top with another layer of salad, ricotta and tomato. Fold back the final layer of pasta and garnish with a little salad and tomato. Repeat with the remaining pasta strips, salad, ricotta and tomato to make four individual servings. Just before serving, drizzle with the balsamic syrup and garnish with parmesan shavings.

Penne Arrabbiata

serves 4

75 g (2¹/₂ oz / ¹/₂ cup) bacon fat
2–3 red chillies
2 tablespoons olive oil
1 large onion, finely chopped
1 garlic clove, finely chopped
500 g (1 lb 2 oz) very ripe tomatoes, finely chopped
500 g (1 lb 2 oz) penne
2 tablespoons chopped flat-leaf (Italian) parsley
grated parmesan or pecorino cheese, to serve

1   Use a large knife to finely chop the bacon fat. Chop the chillies. Heat the oil in a heavy-based pan and add the bacon fat, chilli, onion and garlic. Fry for 8 minutes, stirring occasionally.

2   Add the chopped tomato to the pan with 125 ml (4 fl oz / ¹/₂ cup) of water and season to taste. Cover and simmer for about 40 minutes, or until the sauce is thick and rich.

3   Meanwhile, cook the penne in a saucepan of boiling salted water until *al dente*. Drain and return to the pan to keep warm.

4   Add the parsley to the sauce and toss gently with the pasta. Serve with the parmesan or pecorino cheese sprinkled over the top.

Spinach and Ricotta Gnocchi

Serves 4-6

4 slices white bread, crusts removed
125 ml (4 fl oz/^{1}/2 cup) milk
500 g (1 lb 2 oz) frozen spinach, thawed
250 g (9 oz) ricotta cheese
2 eggs
60 g (2^1/4 oz/^{1}/2 cup) grated parmesan cheese
30 g (1 oz/^{1}/4 cup) plain (all-purpose) flour
shaved parmesan cheese, to serve

GARLIC BUTTER SAUCE
100 g (3^1/2 oz) butter
2 garlic cloves, crushed
3 tablespoons chopped basil
1 ripe tomato, diced

1   Soak the bread in the milk for 10 minutes. Squeeze out any excess milk from the bread. Squeeze out any excess liquid from the spinach.

2   Place the bread, spinach, ricotta, eggs and parmesan in a bowl and mix. Refrigerate, covered, for 1 hour. Fold the flour in well.

3   Roll heaped teaspoons of the mixture into dumplings. Cook the gnocchi in batches in a large saucepan of boiling salted water for about 2 minutes, or until the gnocchi rise to the surface. Transfer to a serving plate and keep warm.

4   To make the sauce, combine all the ingredients in a saucepan and cook over medium heat for 3 minutes, or until the butter is nutty brown. Drizzle over the gnocchi and sprinkle with the parmesan.

Tagliatelle with Roasted Tomato Sauce

Serves 4

1kg (2 lb 4 oz) ripe roma (plum) tomatoes
8 garlic cloves, unpeeled
2 tablespoons olive oil
2 teaspoons dried basil
250 ml (9 fl oz/1 cup) vegetable stock
125 ml (4 fl oz/$1/2$ cup) dry white wine
2 tablespoons balsamic vinegar
500g (1 lb 2 oz) tagliatelle
2 tablespoons grated parmesan cheese

1 Preheat the oven to 180°C (350°F/ Gas 4). Cut the tomatoes in half lengthways and arrange cut side up in a baking dish. Sprinkle with 1 tablespoon water to prevent the tomatoes from sticking. Add the garlic to the dish and drizzle the oil over the tomatoes and garlic. Sprinkle with basil, salt and freshly ground black pepper. Bake for 25 minutes, or until soft. Gently remove from the pan and set aside.

2 Heat the baking dish over low heat and add the stock, white wine and vinegar. Bring to the boil, reduce the heat and simmer for 20 minutes. Roughly chop the tomatoes, retaining all the juices. Squeeze the garlic out of the skin and add the tomato and garlic to the sauce.

3 Cook the tagliatelle in a saucepan of boiling salted water until *al dente*. Drain and return to the pan to keep warm. Serve the sauce over the pasta and sprinkle with parmesan.

Baked Fettucine

Serves 4

500 g (1 lb 2 oz) spinach fettucine
60 g (2¹/₄ oz) butter
1 onion, finely chopped
300 g (10¹/₂ oz) sour cream
250 ml (9 fl oz/1 cup) pouring cream
¹/₄ teaspoon ground nutmeg
60 g (2 oz/¹/₂ cup) grated parmesan cheese
150 g (5¹/₂ oz/1 cup) grated mozzarella cheese

1 Preheat the oven to 180°C (350°F/Gas 4). Cook the fettucine in a saucepan of boiling salted water until *al dente*. Drain and return to the pan to keep warm.

2 Melt the butter in a large saucepan and cook the onion over low heat until tender. Add the pasta. Add the sour cream and toss well. Simmer, stirring, until the pasta is well coated.

3 Stir in the cream, nutmeg and half the parmesan and season well. Pour into a greased ovenproof dish. Sprinkle with the combined mozzarella and remaining parmesan. Bake for 15 minutes, or until golden.

Ravioli Aperto

Serves 4

FILLING
30 g (1 oz) butter
1 small onion, finely chopped
85 g (3 oz) baby English spinach leaves
250 g (9 oz) ricotta cheese
60 g (2¹/₄ oz) thick (double/heavy) cream

8 fresh lasagne sheets
100 g (3¹/₂ oz) frozen spinach, thawed
250 ml (9 fl oz/1 cup) chicken stock

1 To make the filling, melt the butter in a frying pan and add the onion. Cook, stirring, for 5 minutes, or until softened. Add the baby spinach leaves and cook for 4 minutes. Remove from the heat, cool to room temperature and then chop. Add the ricotta and 2 tablespoons of the cream and stir well. Season with salt and pepper.

2 Cook the lasagne, 1–2 sheets at a time, in a saucepan of boiling water until just softened. Remove the sheets carefully with two spatulas or wooden spoons and lay out flat on a damp tea towel (dish towel). Preheat the oven to 180°C (350°F/Gas 4).

3 Cut the lasagne sheets in half. Line a baking tray with baking (parchment) paper and lay out half the pieces of pasta on the tray.

4 Divide the filling into eight portions and spoon a portion into the centre of each square. Place the other eight pasta sheets on top to enclose the filling and cover with a damp tea towel (dish towel).

5   Blend the spinach with a little of the chicken stock until smooth.
    Transfer to a saucepan with the remaining stock and heat for
    2 minutes. Add the remaining cream, stir well, season and remove
    from the heat.

6   Heat the ravioli in the oven for 5 minutes, or until just warm. Place
    two ravioli on each plate. Pour the sauce over the ravioli and
    serve immediately.

Spaghettini Aglio e Olio

Serves 4

400 g (14 oz) spaghettini
90 ml (3 fl oz) olive oil
5 garlic cloves, crushed
pinch of dried chilli flakes
2 tablespoons finely chopped flat-leaf (Italian) parsley
grated pecorino cheese, to serve

1 Cook the pasta in a saucepan of boiling salted water until *al dente*.

2 Meanwhile, heat the oil in a large frying pan over very low heat. Add the garlic and chilli flakes and gently fry for about 2 minutes, or until the garlic has softened but not browned. Remove the frying pan from the heat.

3 Lightly drain the spaghettini. Don't shake it dry in the colander, as you need it to retain a little of the cooking water. Return the frying pan to the heat, add the spaghettini and parsley and toss to coat. Serve with the pecorino.

Fettucine Alfredo

serves 4–6

500 g (1 lb 2 oz) fettucine
90 g (3¼ oz) butter
150 g (5 oz/1½ cups) grated parmesan cheese
315 ml (11 fl oz/1¼ cups) pouring cream
3 tablespoons chopped flat-leaf (Italian) parsley

1   Cook the fettucine in a saucepan of boiling salted water until *al dente*. Drain and return to the pan to keep warm.

2   Meanwhile, melt the butter in a saucepan over low heat. Add the parmesan and cream and bring to the boil, stirring constantly. Reduce the heat and simmer, stirring, until thickened slightly. Add the parsley and salt and pepper and stir well. Add the sauce to the pasta and toss well.

Conchiglie with Chickpeas

Serves 4

250 g (9 oz) dried chickpeas
60 ml (2 fl oz/¼ cup) olive oil
1 large onion, finely chopped
1 celery stalk, finely chopped
1 carrot, finely chopped
2 garlic cloves, crushed
1 rosemary sprig
pinch of crushed dried chilli
2 tablespoons tomato passata (puréed tomatoes)
1.5 litres (52 fl oz/6 cups) vegetable stock
125 g (4½ oz) conchiglie
drizzle of extra virgin olive oil
grated parmesan cheese, to serve

1 Put the chickpeas in a large saucepan, cover with cold water and soak overnight. Drain and rinse under cold water.

2 Heat the olive oil in a large saucepan. Add the chopped vegetables, garlic and rosemary and cook over low heat for 8 minutes. Add the chilli and season. Stir in the tomato passata and stock, then add the chickpeas. Bring to the boil. Reduce the heat and simmer for 1–1½ hours, or until the chickpeas are tender, adding a little boiling water every so often to maintain the level of liquid.

3 Add the pasta and continue cooking until it is *al dente*. Remove the rosemary sprig. Divide among serving plates, drizzle with extra virgin olive oil and sprinkle with parmesan cheese.

Tomato and Ricotta Orecchiette

Serves 4

400 g (14 oz) orecchiette
470 g (1 lb 1 oz) roma (plum) tomatoes
315 g (11 oz) ricotta cheese
45 g (1¹/₂ oz) parmesan cheese, grated, plus extra to serve
8 basil leaves, torn into pieces

1 Cook the orecchiette in a saucepan of boiling salted water until *al dente*. Drain and return to the pan to keep warm.

2 Score a cross in the top of each tomato. Plunge them into boiling water for 20 seconds, then drain and peel the skin away from the cross. Core and chop. Mash the ricotta, add the parmesan and season.

3 Add the ricotta mixture, the tomato and basil to the pasta. Season and toss. Serve with the extra parmesan.

Tagliatelle with Asparagus, Peas and Herb Sauce

Serves 4

375 g (13 oz) tagliatelle

2 leeks, thinly sliced

250 ml (9 fl oz/1 cup) chicken or vegetable stock

3 garlic cloves, crushed

250 g (9 oz/1^{1}/$_{2}$ cups) shelled fresh peas

1 tablespoon finely chopped mint

400 g (14 oz) asparagus spears, cut into 5 cm (2 in) lengths

15 g (^{1}/$_{2}$ oz/^{1}/$_{4}$ cup) finely chopped flat-leaf (Italian) parsley

30 g (1 oz/^{1}/$_{2}$ cup) shredded basil

80 ml (2^{3}/$_{4}$ fl oz/^{1}/$_{3}$ cup) pouring cream

pinch of grated nutmeg

1 tablespoon grated parmesan cheese

2 tablespoons extra virgin olive oil, to serve

1 Cook the tagliatelle in a saucepan of boiling salted water until *al dente*. Drain and return to the pan to keep warm.

2 Put the leeks and 125 ml (4 fl oz/^{1}/$_{2}$ cup) of the stock in a large deep frying pan. Cook over low heat, stirring often, for 4–5 minutes. Stir in the garlic, peas and mint and cook for 1 minute. Add the remaining stock and 125 ml (4 fl oz/^{1}/$_{2}$ cup) water and bring to the boil. Simmer for 5 minutes. Add the asparagus, parsley and basil and season well. Simmer for 3–4 minutes, or until the asparagus is just tender. Gradually increase the heat to thicken the sauce. Stir in the cream, nutmeg and parmesan and season.

3 Add the tagliatelle to the sauce and toss lightly to coat. Divide among four bowls and drizzle with olive oil. Sprinkle with extra grated parmesan to serve.

Penne with Tomato and Onion Jam and Olives

Serves 4

60 ml (2 fl oz/¼ cup) olive oil
4 red onions, sliced
1 tablespoon soft brown sugar
2 tablespoons balsamic vinegar
800 g (1 lb 12 oz) tinned tomatoes
500 g (1 lb 2 oz) penne
150 g (5½ oz) small pitted black olives
75 g (2½ oz/¾ cup) grated parmesan cheese

1 Heat the oil in a non-stick frying pan over medium heat. Add the onion and sugar and cook for 25–30 minutes, or until caramelized.

2 Stir in the vinegar. Bring to the boil and cook for 5 minutes. Add the tomatoes and return to the boil. Reduce the heat to medium–low and simmer for 25 minutes, or until the tomatoes are reduced.

3 Cook the penne in a saucepan of boiling salted water until *al dente*. Drain and return to the pan to keep warm. Add the tomato mixture and olives and stir to combine well. Season to taste with salt and black pepper and garnish with the parmesan.

 Caramelized onions will keep for a few days if covered with oil and stored in the refrigerator.

Roasted Chunky Ratatouille Cannelloni

1 eggplant (aubergine)

2 zucchini (courgettes)

1 large red capsicum (pepper)

1 large green capsicum (pepper)

3–4 ripe roma (plum) tomatoes

12 unpeeled garlic cloves

60 ml (2 fl oz/$1/4$ cup) olive oil

300 ml (10$1/2$ fl oz) tomato passata (puréed tomatoes)

350 g (12 oz) cannelloni tubes

3 tablespoons shredded basil

300 g (10$1/2$ oz) ricotta cheese

100 g (3$1/2$ oz) feta cheese

1 egg, lightly beaten

50 g (1$3/4$ oz) pecorino pepato cheese, grated

1 Preheat the oven to 200°C (400°F/ Gas 6). Cut the eggplant, zucchini, capsicums and tomatoes into 2 cm ($3/4$ in) cubes and place in a baking dish with the garlic. Drizzle with the oil and toss to coat. Bake for 1 hour 30 minutes, or until the vegetables are tender and the tomatoes slightly mushy. Peel and lightly mash the garlic cloves.

2 Pour the passata over the base of a large ovenproof dish. Spoon the ratatouille into the cannelloni tubes and arrange in the dish.

3 Combine the basil, ricotta, feta and egg, season well and spoon over the cannelloni. Sprinkle with the pecorino and bake for 30 minutes, or until the cannelloni are soft.

Fusilli with Broccolini, Chilli and Olives

Serves 4

60 ml (2 fl oz/¼ cup) olive oil
1 onion, finely chopped
3 garlic cloves
1 teaspoon chilli flakes
700 g (1 lb 9 oz) broccolini, cut into 1 cm (½ in) pieces
125 ml (4 fl oz/½ cup) vegetable stock
400 g (14 oz) fusilli
90 g (3¼ oz/½ cup) black olives, pitted and chopped
7 g (¼ oz/¼ cup) finely chopped flat-leaf (Italian) parsley
25 g (1 oz/¼ cup) grated pecorino cheese
2 tablespoons basil leaves, shredded

1 Heat the olive oil in a large non-stick frying pan over medium heat. Cook the onion, garlic and chilli until softened, then add the broccolini and cook for 5 minutes.

2 Meanwhile, cook the fusilli in a saucepan of boiling salted water until *al dente*. Drain and return to the pan to keep warm.

3 When the broccolini is tender, remove from the heat. Add to the pasta with the olives, parsley, pecorino and basil, and season well. Gently toss together and serve immediately.

Conchiglie with Spring Vegetables

500 g (1 lb 2 oz) conchiglie
310 g (11 oz/2 cups) frozen peas
310 g (11 oz/2 cups) frozen broad (fava) beans, blanched and peeled
80 ml (2$^{1}/_{2}$ fl oz/$^{1}/_{3}$ cup) olive oil
6 spring onions (scallions), cut into 3 cm (1$^{1}/_{4}$ in) pieces
2 garlic cloves, finely chopped
250 ml (9 fl oz/1 cup) vegetable or chicken stock
12 thin asparagus spears, cut into 5 cm (2 in) lengths
$^{1}/_{2}$ teaspoon finely grated lemon zest
60 ml (2 fl oz/$^{1}/_{4}$ cup) lemon juice
shaved parmesan cheese, to serve

1 Cook the conchiglie in a saucepan of boiling salted water until *al dente*. Drain and return to the pan to keep warm.

2 Meanwhile, place the peas in a saucepan of boiling water. Cook for 1–2 minutes, or until tender. Remove with a slotted spoon and plunge into cold water. Add the broad beans to the same saucepan of boiling water and cook for 1–2 minutes, then drain and plunge into cold water. Remove and slip the skins off.

3 Heat 2 tablespoons of the oil in a frying pan. Add the spring onion and garlic and cook over medium heat for 2 minutes, or until softened. Pour in the stock and cook for 5 minutes, or until slightly reduced. Add the asparagus and cook for 3–4 minutes, or until bright green and just tender. Stir in the peas and broad beans and cook for 2–3 minutes, or until heated through.

4 Toss the remaining oil through the pasta, then add the vegetables, lemon zest and lemon juice. Season and toss. Serve with parmesan.

Pizzoccheri

Serves 4

PIZZOCCHERI
200 g (7 oz) buckwheat flour
100 g (3½ oz) plain bread flour
1 egg
120 ml (4 fl oz) milk, warmed

CHEESE, POTATO AND CABBAGE SAUCE
350 g (12 oz) savoy cabbage or any other cabbage, roughly chopped
180 g (6½ oz) potatoes, cubed
80 ml (2½ fl oz/⅓ cup) olive oil
1 tablespoon chopped sage
2 garlic cloves, crushed
350 g (12 oz) Italian cheeses, such as fontina or taleggio, cubed
75 g (2½ oz) parmesan cheese, grated

1   To make the pizzoccheri, sift the two flours into a bowl and add a pinch of salt. Make a well in the centre and add the egg. Mix the egg into the flour and then gradually add the milk, mixing continuously until you have a soft dough (you may need more or less milk, depending on the dryness of your flour).

2   Knead the dough for a few minutes, or until elastic, and then cover with a tea towel (dish towel) and allow to rest for 1 hour. Using a pasta machine or a rolling pin, roll out the dough very thinly and cut into noodles about 1 cm (½ in) wide.

3 To make the sauce, bring a large saucepan of salted water to the boil. Add the cabbage and potato and cook for 3–5 minutes, or until cooked through. Add the pizzoccheri and cook for a further 2 minutes. Drain, reserving 250 ml (9 fl oz/1 cup) of the cooking water.

4 Heat the oil in a saucepan and gently cook the sage and garlic for 1 minute. Add the cheese cubes and mix briefly, then add the cabbage, potato and pizzoccheri and season with salt and pepper. Remove from the heat and gently stir the mixture together, adding some pasta water to loosen it a little. Serve immediately with the parmesan sprinkled on top.

This buckwheat pasta is a classic recipe from Valtellina near the Swiss border and uses the most common foods of that area.

Baked Sweet Potato and Watercress Gnocchi

Serves 6

700 g (1 lb 9 oz) orange sweet potato
300 g (10 1/2 oz) desiree potatoes
350 g (12 oz) plain (all-purpose) flour
35 g (1 1/4 oz / 1/3 cup) grated parmesan cheese
30 g (1 oz / 1 cup) watercress leaves, finely chopped
1 garlic clove, crushed
60 g (2 1/4 oz) butter
25 g (1 oz / 1/4 cup) grated parmesan cheese, extra
2 tablespoons chopped flat-leaf (Italian) parsley

1 Boil the sweet potato and desiree potatoes in their skin until tender. Drain, peel and press through a potato ricer or mouli into a bowl.

2 Add the flour, grated parmesan, watercress and garlic, and season well. Gently bring together with your hands until a soft dough forms. Portion into walnut-size pieces and shape using the back of a fork.

3 Melt the butter in a large roasting tray. Preheat the grill (broiler) to medium–high heat.

4 Cook the gnocchi in a large saucepan of boiling salted water for 2 minutes, or until they rise to the surface. Scoop out with a slotted spoon, draining the water off well. Arrange in the roasting tray, tossing gently in the butter, and grill (broil) for 5 minutes, or until lightly golden. Sprinkle with the extra parmesan and chopped parsley.

Tagliatelle with Truffles

serves 4

135 g (4³/4 oz) butter
1 garlic clove
400 g (14 oz) fresh tagliatelle
60 g (2¹/4 oz) parmesan cheese, grated
1 small white Alba truffle or black Norcia truffle

1. Melt the butter in a saucepan over heat. Add the garlic clove and heat until the butter bubbles, separates and turns lightly golden. Strain the butter.

2. Meanwhile, cook the tagliatelle in a saucepan of boiling salted water until *al dente*. Drain and return to the pan. Add the browned butter and the parmesan. Season with salt and black pepper and toss lightly.

3. Place on warmed plates. Using a mandolin or potato peeler, shave a few very thin slices of the truffle onto each serving.

If you are going to the extravagance of using truffles, don't skimp on the parmesan — use parmigiano reggiano for the best flavour. if you can't get a fresh truffle, use one from a jar, preserved in brine.

Spaghetti with Lemon and Rocket

Serves 4

375 g (13 oz) spaghetti
100 g (3¹/2 oz) rocket (arugula), finely shredded
1 tablespoon finely chopped lemon zest
1 garlic clove, finely chopped
1 small red chilli, seeded and finely chopped
1 teaspoon chilli oil
100 ml (3¹/2 fl oz) extra virgin olive oil
60 g (2¹/4 oz) parmesan cheese, finely grated

1 Cook the spaghetti in a saucepan of boiling salted water until *al dente*. Drain and return to the pan to keep warm.

2 Combine the rocket, lemon zest, garlic, chilli, chilli oil, extra virgin olive oil and two-thirds of the grated parmesan in a large bowl and mix together.

3 Add the pasta to the rocket and lemon mixture and stir together well. Serve topped with the remaining parmesan and season to taste with salt and cracked black pepper.

Sweet Potato Ravioli

Serves 4

500 g (1 lb 2 oz) orange sweet potato, chopped
2 teaspoons lemon juice
190 g (6³/4 oz) butter
50 g (1³/4 oz/¹/2 cup) grated parmesan cheese
1 tablespoon chopped chives
1 egg, lightly beaten
250 g (9 oz) packet won ton wrappers
2 tablespoons sage, torn
2 tablespoons chopped walnuts

1 Cook the sweet potato and lemon juice in boiling water for 15 minutes, or until tender. Drain and pat dry with paper towels. Allow to cool for 5 minutes.

2 Blend the sweet potato and 30 g (1 oz) of the butter in a food processor until smooth. Add the parmesan, chives and half the egg. Season and allow to cool completely.

3 Put 2 teaspoons of the mixture in the centre of half the won ton wrappers. Brush the edges with the remaining egg, then cover with the remaining wrappers. Press the edges firmly to seal. Using a 7 cm (2³/4 in) cutter, cut the ravioli into circles.

4 Melt the remaining butter in a small saucepan over low heat and cook until golden brown. Remove from the heat.

5 Cook the ravioli in batches in a saucepan of boiling salted water until *al dente*. Drain and divide with the butter and sprinkled with the sage and walnuts.

Red Lentil and Ricotta Lasagne

Serves 6

125 g (4 oz/1/2 cup) red lentils
2 teaspoons olive oil
2–3 garlic cloves, crushed
1 large onion, chopped
1 small red capsicum (pepper), chopped
2 zucchini (courgettes), sliced
1 celery stalk, sliced
850 g (1 lb 14 oz) tinned chopped tomatoes
2 tablespoons tomato paste (concentrated purée)
1 teaspoon dried oregano
350 g (12 oz) ricotta cheese
12 lasagne sheets
60 g (2 1/4 oz) cheddar cheese, grated

WHITE SAUCE
40 g (1 1/4 oz/1/3 cup) cornflour
750 ml (26 fl oz/3 cups) skim milk
1/4 onion
1/2 teaspoon ground nutmeg

1   Soak the lentils in boiling water for 30 minutes, then drain.
    Meanwhile, heat the oil in a large saucepan. Add the garlic and onion
    and cook for 2 minutes. Add the capsicum, zucchini and celery and
    cook for 2–3 minutes.

2   Add the lentils, tomato, tomato paste, oregano and 375 ml
    (13 fl oz/1 1/2 cups) water. Bring slowly to the boil, reduce the heat
    and simmer for 30 minutes, or until the lentils are tender.

3 To make the white sauce, blend the cornflour with 2 tablespoons of the milk until smooth. Pour the remaining milk into the pan, add the onion and stir over low heat until the mixture boils and thickens. Add the nutmeg and pepper, then cook over low heat for 5 minutes. Remove the onion.

4 Beat the ricotta with about 125 ml (4 fl oz/½ cup) of the white sauce. Preheat the oven to 180°C (350°F/Gas 4). Spread one-third of the lentil mixture over the base of a 3 litre (104 fl oz/12 cup) ovenproof dish. Cover with a layer of lasagne sheets. Spread another third of the lentil mixture over the pasta, then spread the ricotta evenly over the top. Follow with another layer of lasagne, then the remaining lentils. Pour the white sauce evenly over the top and sprinkle with the grated cheese. Bake for 1 hour, covering loosely with foil if the top starts to brown too much.

Balsamic Capsicum on Angel Hair

Serves 4

300 g (10¹/₂ oz) angel hair pasta
2 red capsicums (peppers)
2 yellow capsicums (peppers)
2 green capsicums (peppers)
4 garlic cloves, crushed
2 tablespoons orange juice
80 ml (2¹/₂ fl oz/¹/₃ cup) balsamic vinegar
100 g (3¹/₂ oz) goat's cheese
15 g (¹/₂ oz/¹/₂ cup) basil

1 Cook the pasta in a saucepan of boiling salted water until *al dente*. Drain and return to the pan to keep warm.

2 Cut the capsicums into large flat pieces and place under a hot grill (broiler) until the skins blister and blacken. Leave to cool in a plastic bag, then peel away the skin and cut the flesh into thin strips.

3 Combine the capsicum strips, garlic, orange juice and balsamic vinegar. Drizzle over the pasta and gently toss.

4 Serve topped with crumbled goat's cheese and basil and a sprinkling of cracked black pepper.

Fettucine with Creamy Spinach and Roast Tomato

Serves 4-6

6 roma (plum) tomatoes
40 g (1½ oz) butter
2 garlic cloves, crushed
1 onion, chopped
500 g (1 lb 2 oz) English spinach, trimmed
250 ml (9 fl oz/1 cup) vegetable stock
125 ml (4 fl oz/½ cup) thick (double/heavy) cream
500 g (1 lb 2 oz) fresh spinach fettucine
50 g (1¾ oz) shaved parmesan cheese

1　Preheat the oven to 220°C (425°F/ Gas 7). Cut the tomatoes in half lengthways, then cut each half into three wedges. Place the wedges on a lightly greased baking tray and bake for 30–35 minutes, or until softened and slightly golden.

2　Meanwhile, heat the butter in a large frying pan. Add the garlic and onion and cook over medium heat for 5 minutes, or until the onion is soft. Add the spinach, stock and cream, increase the heat to high and bring to the boil. Simmer rapidly for 5 minutes.

3　While the spinach mixture is cooking, cook the fettucine in a saucepan of boiling salted water until *al dente*. Drain and return to the pan to keep warm. Remove the spinach mixture from the heat and season well. Cool slightly, then process in a food processor until smooth. Toss through the pasta until well coated. Divide among serving bowls and top with the roasted tomatoes and parmesan.

Spaghetti Napolitana

Serves 4-6

2 tablespoons olive oil
1 onion, finely chopped
1 carrot, finely chopped
1 celery stick, finely chopped
500 g (1 lb 2 oz) very ripe tomatoes, chopped
2 tablespoons chopped flat-leaf (Italian) parsley
2 teaspoons sugar
500 g (1 lb 2 oz) spaghetti

1 Heat the oil in a heavy-based saucepan. Add the onion, carrot and celery. Cover and cook for 10 minutes over low heat, stirring occasionally.

2 Add the tomato to the pan with the parsley, sugar and 125 ml (4 fl oz/½ cup) of water. Bring to the boil, reduce the heat to low, cover and simmer for 45 minutes, stirring occasionally. Season to taste. If necessary, add up to 185 ml (6 fl oz/¾ cup) more water if the sauce needs thinning.

3 Cook the spaghetti in a saucepan of boiling salted water until *al dente*. Drain and return to the pan. Toss gently with the sauce.

Casarecci with Roasted Tomatoes, Rocket and Goat's Cheese

Serves 4

16 roma (plum) tomatoes

7 g (¹/₄ oz/¹/₄ cup) basil leaves, torn

400 g (14 oz) casarecci

80 ml (2¹/₂ fl oz/¹/₃ cup) olive oil

2 garlic cloves, finely sliced

2 tablespoons lemon juice

120 g (4 oz/4 cups) rocket (arugula), roughly chopped

2 tablespoons chopped flat-leaf (Italian) parsley

35 g (1¹/₄ oz/¹/₃ cup) grated parmesan cheese

100 g (3¹/₂ oz) goat's cheese

1 Preheat the oven to 160°C (315°F/Gas 2–3). Score a cross in the base of the tomatoes. Place in a heatproof bowl and cover with boiling water. Leave for 30 seconds, then transfer to cold water and peel the skin away from the cross. Cut in half and place cut side up on a wire rack over a baking tray. Season and scatter with the basil leaves. Put the tray in the oven and bake for 3 hours.

2 Cook the casarecci in a saucepan of boiling salted water until *al dente*. Drain and return to the pan to keep warm.

3 Heat the olive oil and garlic over medium heat until it just begins to sizzle. Remove and add to the pasta with the tomatoes, lemon juice, rocket, parsley and parmesan. Stir gently to combine, allowing the heat from the pasta to wilt the rocket. Serve topped with crumbled goat's cheese.

Herb-filled Ravioli

Serves 4

300 g (10¹/2 oz) plain (all-purpose) flour
3 eggs, beaten
60 ml (2 fl oz/¹/4 cup) oil
250 g (9 oz/1 cup) ricotta cheese
2 tablespoons grated Parmesan cheese
2 teaspoons chopped chives
1 tablespoon chopped flat-leaf (Italian) parsley
2 teaspoons chopped basil
1 teaspoon chopped lemon thyme or thyme
1 egg, beaten, extra

1   Sift the flour into a bowl and make a well in the centre. Gradually mix in the eggs and oil. Turn out onto a lightly floured surface and knead for 6 minutes, or until smooth. Cover with plastic wrap and leave for 30 minutes.

2   To make the filling, mix the ricotta, parmesan and herbs. Season well.

3   Divide the dough into four portions and shape each into a log. Keeping the unworked portions covered, take one portion and flatten it with one or two rolls of a rolling pin. With machine rollers set to the widest setting, crank the dough through two or three times. Fold it into thirds, turn the dough by 90 degrees and feed it through again. If the dough feels sticky, flour it lightly each time it is rolled. Repeat the rolling and folding 8–10 times until the dough feels smooth and elastic. Reduce the width of the rollers by one setting and pass the dough through without folding it. Repeat, setting the rollers one

notch closer each time until you have reached a thickness of 2 mm (⅙ in). Roll another sheet slightly larger than the first and cover with a tea towel.

4 Spread the smaller sheet out onto a work surface. Spoon 1 teaspoon of the filling at 5 cm (2 in) intervals. Brush the beaten egg between the filling along the cutting lines. Place the larger sheet on top. Press the two sheets together along the cutting line. Cut the ravioli with a pastry wheel or knife. Transfer to a lightly floured baking tray. Repeat with the remaining dough and filling.

5 Cook the ravioli in a saucepan of boiling salted water for 5–8 minutes and top with a sauce of your choice.

Uncooked ravioli can be stored in the refrigerator for 1–2 days.

index